What People ... Christophe

For my daughters, our forthcoming trip to Botswana was a source of such excitement, they could barely sleep for weeks. I wasn't able to sleep either, but from terror rather than anticipation. The possible joys of seeing lions and leopards in their natural habitat paled in comparison with my dread of flying overnight in economy on a notoriously turbulent route. The day after working with Chris, we all flew to Botswana. The flight was pretty bumpy. In fact, the plane ran into three storms on the way; but I wasn't aware of them, as I slept through the night. No big deal for most people; but for me, it was a minor miracle, and it's still working. **LYDIA SLATER – DEPUTY EDITOR, HARPER'S BAZAAR**

Just four days after my session with Christopher, I boarded a 12-hour flight to Puerto Vallarta, Mexico. At the airport, I felt an unusual sense of calm going through customs, took my seat quite happily, and chatted away with my friends as the flight took off (which I didn't give a second thought about). **EMMY GRIFFITHS – HELLO MAGAZINE**

Since seeing Christopher, I can honestly say he has changed my life. My anxiety levels have been substantially reduced, and I now have so many new thinking techniques that I use daily. I would encourage everyone to see Christopher because he has transformed my life. **POPPY JAMIE – TV PRESENTER**

Chris is always there when I need help, his methods have had a positive effect on my wellbeing. **SUKI WATERHOUSE – MODEL, ACTRESS, CELEBRITY**

Within weeks of seeing Christopher, I flew to Los Angeles and back again. 20 hours of flying with no anxiety, no worries and no fear. It was one of the best flights (twice!). I was relaxed and even enjoyed it. It was unbelievable. I never imagined that it would be possible… and it was! Thank you, Chris. You made the seemingly impossible very, very, possible! **ALEX SEGAL – ACTING AGENT**

Since the last time I met Chris, I've travelled quite a bit and have done a lot of flying. Before I met him, when I felt turbulence, especially over water, I would think about drowning. Now I don't think about that, and I feel better about flying. **JENNIFER BENAVIDEZ – DANCE INSTRUCTOR**

I had previously tried hypnosis and airline Fear of Flying courses in order to try to alleviate my fear. I had spent over £1000.00 and, sadly, without success. I was not convinced Chris could help, despite seeing his very impressive results on YouTube. After one hour with Chris, I left feeling very 'zen' and content! On my next flight, to my great surprise, I felt so much better! I have flown tens of times since and each time I feel fine. **SUSAN LAWTON – SALES MANAGER**

Working with Chris was unlike anything I had experienced before. I have been on two flights – to Berlin and to Rhodes, and they were absolutely fine – I have never been so relaxed on flights. **JENNIFER HOWARD-DOBSON – SOLICITOR**

I used to be terrified of turbulence when flying, then I worked with Christopher, and now I get so happy when there might be turbulence, I actually look forward to it. **AREZOO KAVIANI – CELEBRITY BEAUTY THERAPIST**

Just two weeks after my session with Chris, I took a flight from London to Malaysia that lasted 14 hours. During the two weeks in Malaysia, I took three internal flights, two of which were on small light aircraft. The change in me was incredible. My partner, who usually witnesses the anxiety and stress I face, couldn't believe the change. Since then, I have taken many flights, and I have suffered very little anxiety. **KATE LLOYD – MARKETING DIRECTOR AT VEHICLE WEIGHING SOLUTIONS LTD**

A week later, I was due to fly to America. It was a nine-hour flight, which before would have filled me with anxiety and dread. The most amazing thing was that I enjoyed the flight. Take off, mid-air and landing had no impact on me, and it was an exhilarating feeling to no longer have any irrational thoughts or fears. **NICK COOKE – STUDENT OF LONDON FASHION**

F@C#
YOUR FEAR
OF FLYING

*The Proven Approach to Break Through
Your Flying Phobia and Enjoy Travel,
Even If Everything Else Has Failed*

Christopher Paul Jones

The Breakthrough Expert

BrightFlame Books, Toronto

Copyright © 2020 by Christopher Paul Jones. All rights reserved.

Illustrations by Jess Anastasi and Amelia Anastasi

Book design by BrightFlame Books

Editor Rob Cuesta

First Edition. Published in Canada by BrightFlame Books, Burlington, Ontario. www.BrightFlameBooks.com

No part of this book may be used or reproduced in any manner whatsoever without written permission except in the case of brief quotations embodied in critical reviews and articles in their entirety.

Limit of Liability/Disclaimer of Warranty: The information in this book is presented for entertainment purposes only. The publisher and authors make no representations or warranties with respect to the accuracy or completeness of the information contained in this work and specifically disclaim any implied warranties of merchantability or fitness for a particular purpose. No warranty may be created or extended by sales representatives or written sales materials. The advice and strategies contained herein may not be suitable for your situation. You should consult with a qualified professional adviser where appropriate. Neither the publisher nor the author shall be liable for any loss of income, profit or any other commercial damages, nor any emotional or psychological distress, including but not limited to special, incidental, consequential, or other damages.

TABLE OF CONTENTS

Foreword By Dr Naheed Rana, Geneticist		vii
Disclaimer		ix
Before We Begin		ix
Introduction		xi

PART ONE:
FEARS, PHOBIAS, AND ANXIETY

Chapter One	Flying Phobia: The Top 10 Myths Debunked	3
Chapter Two	What is a Phobia?	11
Chapter Three	Introducing The Integrated Change System	33

PART TWO:
SEVEN ACTION STEPS TO BREAK THROUGH YOUR FLYING PHOBIA

Chapter Four	Action Step 1: Relax the Conscious Mind and Body	43
Chapter Five	Action Step 2: Get Precision	51
Chapter Six	Action Step 3: Find the Benefit Behind your Phobia	61
Chapter Seven	Action Step 4: Uncover the Strategy of your Phobia	75
Chapter Eight	Action Step 5: Transforming the Past	103
Chapter Nine	Action Step 6: Change your Stimulus-Response	113
Chapter Ten	Action Step 7: Designing Your Fear-Free Future	119
Chapter Eleven	Preparing for Your Flight	129
	Conclusion	135
	Reader Resources	136

FOREWORD

By Dr Naheed Rana, Geneticist

How often do you meet someone who can change your life? Not often at all! I have been very fortunate to cross paths with an exceptional, professional and passionate individual who really has changed my life! Christopher Paul Jones not only defies any challenge that looks impossible, but he has the insight and expertise to open your eyes and your mind to alternative solutions to any problem.

Christopher's approach may come across as being New Age, but as a Doctor in Genetics, Epidemiology, and Public Health, I was curious about how my brain chemistry could change using his system. I had to believe it when it did really happen to me. Christopher combines many different types of psychotherapies and behavioural therapies to develop a unique integrated approach which is so precisely designed that my phobia of dogs, which I have had since I was a little girl was completely cured in one afternoon! No pills, no medication, just the incredible Christopher. I am now able to run past dogs, stroke dogs and even hang around a whole bunch of dogs in a park which is something I have struggled with all my life – until now. All the techniques that Chris has gone through and taught me have put this amazing confidence into me.

Having explored the scientific basis and impact, I would advocate this method to anyone determined to overcome a phobia. Christopher's approach is beyond belief, and I firmly believe there is a huge need for this method to be utilised at a personal level and more broadly in the healthcare arena. I am confident that by reading this book, you will open the gates of your mind and achieve what you thought could not be possible. Try it and enjoy the ride!

DISCLAIMER

Before We Begin

Some client names and identifying details have been changed to protect the privacy of individuals unless express permission has been given by them to use their real names.

Although the author has made every effort to ensure that the information in this book was correct at time of publication, the author does not assume and hereby disclaims any liability to any party for any loss, damage, or disruption caused by errors or omissions. This book is not intended as a substitute for professional advice and support.

Introduction

I wasn't always a therapist helping people overcome flying phobias. In fact, there was a time when I, too, was afraid of flying just like you.

Many years ago, I was a video cameraman and one of my assignments was a documentary about snowboarders. This was in the days before camera drones, so when the director asked for aerial footage of a group of snowboarders coming down a hill, it meant getting in a helicopter to film it. At that time, I wasn't yet scared of flying, so I jumped in. And I don't mind telling you, I got some great shots.

It was the last day of the shoot, so that night, after we landed, everyone went to the pub to celebrate, and the next day we flew home.

A few weeks later, we went back for what we call a 'pick up', which is where you take additional shots for the documentary that you couldn't get the first time around. At the hotel, I heard someone say that the helicopter I had flown in on my last visit had crashed just 30 minutes after dropping me off in town.

At first, I didn't think much about it. After all, an accident could happen any time, so what difference did it make whether it was thirty minutes after it dropped me off or a week later.

But the next day I was out with the snowboarders having fun on the mountain when one of them became very serious and pointed over towards a black streak down the side of a nearby mountain. "You see those scorch marks?" he said. "That's where your helicopter crashed into the mountain last time. Man, you were so lucky you got off it when you did."

As I stared at the blackened snow and the charred tree stumps, the image burned itself deep into my subconscious, and I thought, *That could have been me.*

After that, I couldn't even get on an aeroplane. But whenever I tried to explain to my friends and family why I couldn't fly somewhere with them, no one seemed to understand. Well-meaning friends, family members, and colleagues would produce what they thought were helpful statistics in a bid to help me get over my phobia.

"Look," they'd say, "you're more likely to get hit by a bus than you are to die in an aircraft." Or "You've got as much chance of a supermarket ceiling falling on your head as you have of dying in an air crash." While those statistics might have made me afraid to cross the road or go shopping, however, they did absolutely nothing to reduce my fear of flying. I knew my fear of flying didn't make sense, but that didn't stop my heart from racing at the sight or sound of an aircraft. And it didn't stop my palms from becoming sweaty, or my breathing turning rapid.

My own story illustrates just how quickly a fear of flying can develop. But the good news is, you can get rid of it equally fast. If the brain can learn to go from joy to fear in a moment, the reverse must also be true: you can go from fear to pleasure just as quickly. You just need to know what (metaphorical) buttons to press.

Which is how I finally overcame my own fear of flying some years later.

Like many people with a flying phobia, I learned to get by. I coped. I even convinced myself that vacations at home were every bit as good as a holiday in some far-flung sunny resort. And when something came up that absolutely needed me to fly, I'd find a way to get out of it.

And that worked for several years. But one day, out of the blue, I went through an experience in my personal life that made me realise I needed to take control—I call it my lightbulb moment—and I knew that I had to change. I just realised that if I didn't do something, I would always be a victim of my fear.

So, I became a passionate student of the human psyche and learned many forms of therapy and changework: Cognitive Behavioural Therapy (CBT), Hypnotherapy, Neuro-Linguistic Programming (NLP), EMDR, psychotherapy, mindfulness, and many others.

> The result? Well, aside from a list of qualifications as long as your arm, I cured my phobia. And it's hard to describe just how surreal it feels—and at the same time amazing—to sit in the open door of a helicopter looking down at the landscape rushing by. Yet that's precisely what I did after I overcame my flying phobia.

Curing my own problem started me down the road to becoming a therapist. I realised that if I had done it for myself, I could do it for others. So, I took what I'd learned, and my experience of what works and what doesn't work, and today I am Harley Street's leading expert on phobias. I have been featured on the BBC, GQ magazine, Hello magazine, and I count models, movie stars, and celebrities among my clients. Thousands of people have walked through my doors who were absolutely terrified of flying, yet they leave completely free from it—sometimes in minutes.

> *After working with Christopher, my flight on Friday was a success! There were no tears or nervousness at all. It's still hard to explain, and I'm still trying to take it all in. When I got on the plane instead of a wave of anxiety, I felt a wave of confidence and excitement. We even had some turbulence towards the end of the flight and it didn't bother me at all (I even smiled!!).* **Sarah Howley – worked with Christopher on BBC Two's Skies Above Britain**

I have seen how a phobia stopped people from truly living their life, and the world of opportunities that opened up when they freed themselves from the struggle.

In the course of working with phobias over the years, I have met many clients who had tried unsuccessfully to overcome their fear intellectually, with information and statistics, and then beat themselves up for still being afraid. The problem with the logical approach is that the part of the mind that deals with emotion doesn't work on logic.

In this book, I present The Integrated Change System™, a fast and effective method I created to understand and, more importantly, remove your phobia of flying and get back in control of your life.

You will probably find my approach different from that in other books you've read and courses you've attended. Where some of them may include a few psychology tools but focus on trying to teach you how to not be afraid, this book focuses mostly on those tools and how to use them to change your mind and your mindset permanently.

However deeply entrenched your problem is—and however overwhelming your fears and phobias may seem right now—you will find this book is filled with tips and techniques to help you conquer your fear of flying. Take heart: there is a solution!

It's human nature to try to avoid what we fear, but you will find that when you allow yourself to examine your fears and phobias, it will be much easier to let go. The exercises in this book will help you to identify the patterns of behaviour and thought that you are running which have created the phobia, and I will share with you techniques that will help you to make changes and come up with new ways of thinking and behaving.

Phobias can be traumatic and scary, but the good thing is, that makes them easy to spot. If someone tells you to get on a plane, but instead of getting on it you scream ,"No! Get away from me!" you can be pretty sure you have a flying phobia.

PART ONE
Fears, Phobias, and Anxiety

CHAPTER ONE

Flying Phobia: The Top 10 Myths Debunked

Many "Cure your flying phobia" books and workshops start by looking at the myths and misconceptions that have arisen around flying, and you're probably expecting the same from this book. So, let's look at ten of the most common myths that surround flying and flight safety, then we'll get into the real work of dealing with your fears!

Myth 1: "Flying is dangerous!"

In reality, compared to other forms of transport, flying is the safest way to travel. The actual risk of being killed in an air crash is anywhere from 1 in 5,000,000 to 1 in 20,000,000[1]. To put that in context, according to The Guardian, you are 100 times more likely to die travelling in a car or truck than in a plane[2]. In fact, more people are killed by lightning strikes each year than die in plane crashes, and in some years *there are <u>no deaths</u> in commercial aviation incidents at all.*

---

[1] https://www.newsweek.com/what-are-odds-dying-plane-crash-app-892008
[2] https://www.theguardian.com/world/2011/sep/05/september-11-road-deaths

Myth 2: "It has to happen to somebody!"

Each year, 55.3 million people die around the world, which is about 8 people out of every 1,000.[3] But only a tiny fraction of those die in airplane accidents. In fact, the fear of flying is far more likely to kill you than flying itself. And I'm not just talking about the health effects of fear and stress: after the attack on the World Trade Center, large numbers of Americans switched from flying to driving, and as a result, in the 12 months after 9/11, almost 1,600 more people died on the roads.[4]

If you're going to argue "it has to happen to somebody", you should be more worried about mosquitoes (1 in 55), alcohol and drugs (1 in 34), or heart disease (kills 1 in 4 people).

Myth 3: "If an aeroplane crashes it's over—you can't walk away. A least in a car accident there's a chance you'll get out alive."

Fatal plane crashes in which everyone dies make for great news headlines, but they are incredibly rare. In fact, according to the US National Transportation Safety Board, you have a 95.7% chance of walking away from a plane crash.[5]

---

[3] https://www.ecology.com/birth-death-rates/
[4] https://www.theguardian.com/world/2011/sep/05/september-11-road-deaths
[5] https://www.ibtimes.com/after-air-algerie-ah5017-incident-statistical-look-probability-chances-dying-plane-crash-1638206

Myth 4: "Airlines aren't affected by crashes, so they don't care."

Even the cheapest commercial airliners cost upwards of $80 million[6] and compensation costs in the wake of an airplane accident can also run to millions. So, it's a mistake to assume that airlines don't feel any "pain" in the event of a crash. Beyond that, though, remember that behind the logos are human beings who feel guilt and remorse when something happens to their customers.

Myth 5: "If an engine fails, the plane will fall from the sky."

Have you ever thought about gliders? They're planes without engines and yet they fly. It's not the engines that keep a plane up, it's the movement of air over the wings. So, even if all the engines on an airliner were to fail at the same time (which is almost unheard of), it would just become a big glider. Indeed, a plane flying at typical cruising altitude (36,000 feet) could glide 60 miles without engines.[7]

Commercial pilots practice gliding the plane all the time – every time an airliner lands, there's a part of the descent where the pilots reduce the engine power to minimum and allow the momentum of the plane to take them in. So, even if your worst nightmare does happen and the engine

---

[6] https://www.telegraph.co.uk/travel/travel-truths/how-to-buy-an-aircraft-boeing-cost/
[7] https://www.flightdeckfriend.com/what-happens-if-all-the-engines-on-the-p

cuts out, relax safe in the knowledge that your pilot has had rigorous training that taught them to land this big glider.

Myth 6: "Turbulence is dangerous."

Have you ever watched water in a stream? The water is continually moving, but although it flows in a single *general* direction ("downstream"), it doesn't all move at the same rate and in the same exact direction. Which is why, if you look carefully, you see little whorls and eddies in the water. And if you come to a point where two streams meet, the water gets even more turbulent.

The air around a plane is exactly the same. It's full of currents and air streams, some of it moving at different speeds and some in different directions. And just like the whorls and eddies in a stream, when two masses of air moving differently meet, they create turbulence.

Turbulence to a pilot is like waves to the captain of a boat. It's just part of flying. When your plane enters that turbulent patch, it can seem scary, but the worst that's likely to happen is you'll end up with a glass of wine in your lap. [8]

Myth 7: "Lightning can bring down a plane."

While lightning does hit planes on occasions, modern aircraft are designed to withstand it. Indeed, no modern commercial aircraft has been brought down by lightning[9]. So, if lightning does strike, sit

---

[8] https://swissfamilytravel.com/blog/understandinturbulence
[9] https://www.scientificamerican.com/article/what-happens-when-lightni/

back and enjoy the view; it can be pretty spectacular seeing things from that height!

Myth 8: "The wing of the plane might fall off."

Having the wings fall off in mid-air is *highly* unlikely. Planes are designed to allow the wings to bend, and the wings are stress tested before an aircraft is even allowed to fly. In one flex test, the wings of a Boeing 787 were flexed 25 feet upwards – the equivalent of 150% of the most extreme forces a plane would ever be expected to  encounter in normal operation – and the wings stayed firmly attached![10]

Myth 9: "Worrying keeps me in control and prepares me for the 'what if'."

You can't control everything; trying to do so simply creates stress and OCD, and the link between stress and heart attacks is well documented.

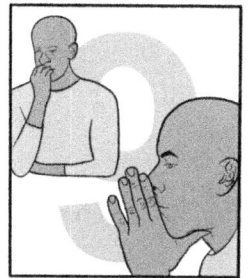 So, unless you want to perhaps die of a heart attack (much more likely than from flying), the best thing that you can do is to seek help for your phobia so that you can soon stop worrying.

---

[10] https://www.wired.com/2010/03/boeing-787-passes-incredible-wing-flex-test/

Myth 10: "If flying is so safe, why do I keep seeing plane crashes on the news."

A few years ago, I was browsing Facebook, and someone had shared a video of a plane crash. It was a small plane; even so, six people had died. The video had been shared by thousands of people and it had millions of views. Sometime later,  I was walking down my street and the end had been cordoned off by the police. When I got home, the tape was gone and the road was back to normal. I tried searching the web to find out what had happened, but I couldn't find anything. Eventually, a few days later, a neighbour told me there had been a serious car crash and six people had died. Here's the thing. If I hadn't been walking down the street that day, I probably wouldn't even have found out about the car crash, even though just as many people died. No-one shared videos of it all over Facebook. The press and TV didn't show scary headlines about it. It barely registered.

Why? Because people die in car crashes all the time.

Flying is so safe, on the other hand, that when there is an incident, it's major news, and those accidents tend to stay in the headlines for several days afterwards, which makes them seem even worse.

In reality, however, there are over 100,000 flights per day (you can see how many aircraft are in the air at any time at FlightRadar.com), and only one fatal accident for every 3 million flights according to the latest aviation safety statistics.[11]

---

[11] https://www.cnbc.com/2019/01/02/fatalities-on-commercial-passenger-aircraft-rise-in-2018.html

Why Statistics Don't Matter

Now that I've cleared up those common misconceptions, do you feel any better? Has it lessened your fear? Are you ready to jump on a plane?

Probably not, because while I've just given you many logical reasons not to be afraid of flying, *phobias aren't logical*. That's why many books and workshops about flying phobia fail: because it doesn't matter how much I show you that flying is safe—unless we sort out what's going on in your mind to create that phobia, your mind isn't going to let go of it.

As you'll learn in this book, a phobia is an *irrational* fear, and that can make it all the more frustrating for the person who is experiencing it, because on a logical level, they know their fear may not have any substance behind it, and that it is based on emotion rather than logic.

The Big Lesson Here

The real reason I wanted to debunk those myths wasn't that I thought it would magically cure you of your phobia.

Often, people who are afraid of flying try to justify their phobia with those myths and others like them. By showing you that those myths are just that – myths – I wanted you to see that when you look at a flying phobia rationally and focus on facts and figures, you very quickly come face to face with the stark truth that your phobia is not founded in reality.

So, if the roots of your phobia aren't rational, where does that phobia come from? That's the topic of the next chapter.

CHAPTER TWO

What is a Phobia?

"I don't have a fear of flying; I have a fear of crashing." – **Billy Bob Thornton**

I was working with a client a few years ago who told me he was in the armed forces, but wouldn't say exactly which branch. After trying to get it out of him for a while, I jokingly asked him, "Are you in the Special Forces or something?"

He looked at me without flinching and said, "I can't tell you."

Keeping up what I thought was a joke, I replied, "You mean you could tell me, but you'd have to kill me?"

I'd expected him to laugh, or at least chuckle. Nothing—not even a smile. Instead, he just repeated, "I can't tell you."

Needless to say, I very quickly dropped that line of enquiry!

Later, however, he did tell me about a time he'd been shot at by the enemy. "We were running back to the helicopter, and bullets were flying everywhere. I was terrified."

I said, "that's not surprising or irrational; anyone would be terrified of being shot at."

He looked at me like I was crazy. "I wasn't scared of being shot. I'm trained to deal with that. It was the idea of getting into the helicopter that terrified me."

Think about that: he was more scared of getting into a helicopter that would take him to safety than he was of being shot.

The Neuroscience of Fear

Later in the book, we'll see that many phobias are created by an event in your past that you may not even be consciously aware of. In that moment, however, your brain linked fear or danger to something. For example, you get chased by a dog, your brain thinks, "how do I feel about this?" and in that moment it creates a connection that all dogs equal fear, After that, whenever you see a dog, it fires off that same fearful response.

That process is critical to how phobias are created, and it's critical to getting rid of them. So let's look a little more deeply at the neuroscience of what's happening in your brain. Or perhaps I should say your brain<u>S</u>. You see, we have three brains (even though you may look at some people and struggle to believe they have even one!).

To explain what's going on, I'll use a model called the *triune brain* ("triune" is just a fancy word for "three parts") which describes how our brains have evolved over time.

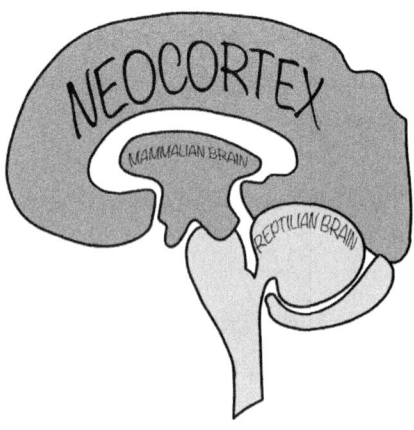

If you were to split a human brain down the middle, you'd find different layers, rather like an archaeological dig. Working from the outside in, there are three layers, each of which developed at different stages in our evolution.

The outermost—and newest—layer of the brain is the *neocortex*. It's the part that makes us human, and it's responsible for language, imagination, abstract thought, and logical reasoning. It's the part we'd like to think is in control but hardly ever is because all that logic and reasoning take time and effort.

Next down from the neocortex is what's called the *mammalian brain* or *limbic system*. This is the part that records (and recalls) memories, creates our emotional responses, and makes value judgements. These are all things that have a significant influence on what we do and how we act, but sometimes we just don't have time to figure out how we truly feel about something.

Deep beneath both of these is the oldest part of the brain, which we call the *reptilian brain*. The job of this part of the brain is to keep you alive, and it does most of this without conscious effort. It's the part that tells your lungs to expand and contract when you breathe without you having to think about it consciously. It pumps your heart, keeps you balanced, regulates your blood pressure, reacts to stress and danger, tells you when to eat, etc. It drives much of our behaviour, using reflexes based on simple rules that it's built up over time to decide what to do. As a result, it usually gets to call the shots, because by the time your neocortex has weighed up all the options and your mammalian brain has decided how you feel about the situation, the reptilian brain has already taken action and moved on.

The survival response: Fight, Flight, or Freeze

Imagine you're a prehistoric human out hunting, and you see a sabre-tooth tiger nearby. You've got a split second to decide what to do.

1. You think, "That tiger looks wounded. I can beat it," and you fight.

2. You think, "It's a bit big, and it has huge teeth. I'd better get out of here," and you run away.

3. You think, "That tiger is probably a lot faster and meaner than I am. There's no way I am going to be able to outrun it," and you play dead.

All of this has to happen in an instant, because if you take too long, the tiger will eat you. So, the reptilian brain doesn't ask the mammalian brain to fish out memories of other times you saw a tiger, and it doesn't ask the neocortex for statistics on "tiger encounter survival rates" or the relative speed of tigers and humans. It simply reacts.

Those three possible responses to danger – to fight, to run away, or to play dead – are nature's oldest and most potent survival strategy, the Fight, Flight, or Freeze Response, and they are controlled by a small, walnut-sized region deep within your reptilian brain called the *amygdala*.

In the split second it takes your amygdala to decide what to do, it also kicks off a series of physiological changes designed to help you survive this situation.

Your pupils dilate so you can see more clearly. Your body hairs stand up so that you are more aware of touch, vibration, and air currents. Your heart beats faster so that more blood is pumped around your body to help your organs work harder. And your breathing speeds up to allow more oxygen into your lungs, nose, and throat to help your limbs work harder.

Your brain knows you are going to need as much energy as possible to help you survive, so it activates fatty cells to create instant energy and shuts down non-essential systems like digestion to conserve energy, which is why when you're afraid your mouth dries up, and you feel a sudden urge to use the toilet.

To minimise potential blood loss in the event of injury, the amygdala also constricts the blood vessels near your skin and draws blood flow away from the surface, making you go pale, and opens your sweat glands to cool your hard-working body, which makes you feel cold and clammy (hence the expression "breaking out in a cold sweat").

Those are all incredibly useful responses when you're facing a sabre-tooth tiger. They're less useful when you're, say, sitting on a plane. Or you see one. Or you just get *close* to one! And yet, that's precisely what the reptilian brain does when you have a fear or phobia.

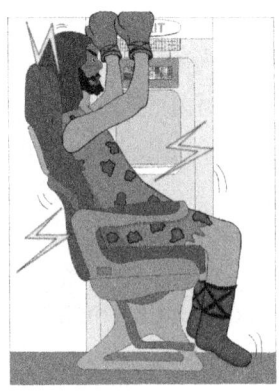

Of course, in a modern setting, the Fight, Flight, or Freeze reactions look very different. If you have a flying phobia, you don't start stabbing flight attendants with your plastic fork or lie on the floor pretending you're dead. Instead, in "Fight" mode, you might get angry and start shouting at cabin crew or loved ones. In "Flight" mode, you might demand to stand up and be let off the plane (if you're going to do that, remember to do it *before* take-off – it's much harder in mid-air!). And in "Freeze" mode you might grab the arms of the seat in the gate area and refuse to get on the plane.

Pavlov? That name rings a bell

In phobias, those reactions are driven by what we call a stimulus-response or anchor. If there was an event in your past which created a fear—for example, a turbulent flight when you were eight years old, or you watched one of your parents be afraid of flying, or you saw a movie about a plane crash one time and it scared you—that trigger goes in deep, and the brain creates a belief that "Flying is dangerous. Flying is scary. I need to avoid it." And because it wants to keep you safe and protected, it decides, *I'm going to react to this. I'm going to help you avoid that, or fight it, or run from it.*

From that time on, whenever you then see an aeroplane—or sit in one, or experience turbulence, or whatever the triggers are for you—your mind goes back in history and asks, "How do I feel about this?" (it happens subconsciously, at lightning speed) and then you react.

You can even see the same things happening with pets. My dog, Lexi, is a very friendly and docile dog, who always wants to play, especially with other dogs. There's a café just outside my house which I pass every day when I take Lexi for a walk, and it has a terrace.

A few years ago, when I moved to the area, I was taking Lexi for her first walk around the new neighbourhood, and there was another dog tied up on the café terrace. As we passed it, it started to snarl and bark at Lexi, obviously looking for a fight. The next time I took Lexi past the café, the dog was there again, and the same thing happened.

Now, I haven't seen that dog since then, but we still pass the café every day on our walk. And every day, as we get close to the terrace, Lexi's tail goes down, and her hair stands up, to show she's ready to defend herself. That's very unusual behaviour for her, and it's interesting that from just two bad experiences she has linked the café to "danger".

Psychologists call these kinds of associations "state-dependent memories" because what triggers us to recall them is actually a state. For example, imagine someone gets so drunk one night that they forget what they did. A few weeks or months later they get very drunk again and they start to remember what happened the last time they were drunk.

The same thing happens for events, places, situations, and other things that you have linked to fear, even if you're not conscious of the link. And when you face a similar occurrence in the future (or even just the possibility that it might happen), your mind and body release stress hormones and you feel the same fear again.

And every time it happens, that fear response is reinforced, creating an anchor, or stimulus-response in a phenomenon known as Pavlovian conditioning.

"Pavlovian" refers to the work of Russian research scientist Ivan Pavlov, and you've probably heard of "Pavlov's dogs". Pavlov noticed that dogs salivate when they eat, so he ran a series of experiments to test whether he could create this response at will in laboratory animals.

He started by ringing a bell and immediately feeding his dogs. Initially, of course, he would ring the bell and then when he fed the dogs, they'd start to salivate. After a while, however, the dogs began to salivate as soon as the bell was rung, before he even fed them. And after more repetitions, he found that he didn't even need to feed the dogs: they would salivate in response to the bell ringing.

Then, in the 1920s, John Watson, a researcher at Johns Hopkins University in the US, decided to see whether humans could be conditioned in the same way as Pavlov's dogs in an infamous piece of research called the "Little Albert" study. Nowadays, the experiment is considered highly controversial and totally unethical by researchers, but it taught us a lot about how phobias are created!

Little Albert was a 9-month-old baby from a local hospital. For the experiment, Watson and his assistant put Albert in the middle of a room and then put a white lab rat near him and let him play with it. Being a baby, Albert had none of the fears and prejudices we feel as humans towards rats, so naturally, he stroked it and played with it.

Once Albert was completely comfortable and happy with the Rat, Watson added a stimulus. Each time Albert went to play with the rat, Watson would make a loud noise. The noise scared Albert and, like any small child that gets a shock, he would start to cry.

Watson and his assistant repeated the process several times until they were sure Albert had been "conditioned". To test the conditioning, they showed Albert the rat again but without the noise. Each time, even though there was no scary noise, Albert got distressed and burst into tears as soon as he saw the rat: the researchers had successfully made him afraid of the rat, even though the poor creature had done nothing to him!

What the Little Albert experiment shows us is that if you expose someone to a negative experience while they are doing something neutral (or even positive, like petting an animal), their subconscious mind takes the negative feelings and associates the whole situation with danger. After that, whenever they are exposed to a similar situation, their subconscious mind goes into overdrive, and its knee-jerk reaction is to try to protect them by any means possible.

> If you add enough shock, fear, or negative emotion to something, you can go from enjoying it to hating it in a moment.

Back when I was a student, there was always too much month left at the end of my money, if you get my meaning, and it felt like every piece of mail that arrived was another bill. Over time, I started to dread the postman, and every time I heard the letterbox, I'd get worried.

I'd anchored all my negative thoughts about money to the sound of the mail being delivered. Many years later, even though money was no longer a problem, I realised I was still getting into that anxious state whenever I heard the letterbox because in my mind I still had that link "letterbox = worry". Had I not noticed the trigger I was running and carried out a process to recondition myself (which I will teach you later in this book), that response to the letterbox would probably still be with me today.

Any sense can become an anchor: a sound, a smell, a taste, something you see (like a facial expression, or an old photo), a texture, etc. Also, bear in mind that anchors can be positive or negative, depending on the original emotion. And just as a negative anchor will put you into a negative state, a positive anchor can put you into a positive state – that's something we use a lot in The Integrated Change System. Here are some typical examples which you've probably experienced for yourself.

- You walk into a room and smell lavender. Suddenly, you're six again, in your grandma's house.
- You're outside, and you catch the smell of a particular perfume. Suddenly you remember a holiday you once had.
- There's probably a song that reminds you of your first kiss, or of kissing the love of your life. And every time you hear it, you smile and remember those happy feelings.
- Or perhaps there's a song that was playing when the love of your life broke up with you. In that case, whenever you hear that song, you probably feel sad. The interesting thing is, you're not always consciously aware of that link. But there's a song that, every time you hear it, you just get very sad and you have no idea why.

So, now let's see how that relates to your fear of flying.

The Power of Conditioning (and Deconditioning!)

While psychologists have known about conditioning for many years, however, it is only in recent times that we created a process for eradicating those anchors, which I will cover in Part Two.

A great example of how powerful these techniques can be is a client who had come to me for something totally unrelated to flying. As we were about to wrap up the session, she said, "You're quite well known for working with flying, aren't you?"

I said, "Yes, I do a lot of work on fear of flying. It is one of my specialities."

She told me she was due to fly the next day and she was terrified of turbulence. Normally, I would spend time working out what the origins of the fear were and looking for what we call the "secondary gain" (which you'll learn about in Chapter Six). However, with only ten minutes left in the session, I didn't have the time for that; so instead, I changed her conditioning.

I asked her to think back to a time when she was happy. I had no idea what she was thinking about specifically, but she suddenly smiled, and her body immediately changed to reflect the powerful emotion she was feeling. I used that emotion to condition her. Then I asked her to think about turbulence and I conditioned that. We repeated the process multiple times and I kept reconditioning thoughts about turbulence while she remembered her happy time.

A few months later, she called me from the airport. "I'm waiting for my flight," she said. "And I'm thinking about turbulence."

At first, I thought that perhaps what we had done hadn't worked and we needed more time to explore it. She quickly stopped me and said, "No, you don't understand. I absolutely love turbulence now. I can't wait for it!"

> You can link pain or pleasure to anything. And if you link enough positive associations to something, it can completely change how you feel.

Conscious vs Subconscious

Earlier, I told you about the triune brain model and described the three "layers" of the brain. There is another way of thinking about how the brain works, and it is one that you're probably aware of, even if you're not really sure what it means in detail.

You've probably heard people talk about the "power of the subconscious (or 'subconscious') mind" and its flipside, the conscious mind.

The conscious mind needs to make sense of what is going on around you. For that, it depends on logic and facts. You spend most of your time thinking consciously: in school, at university, and at work (unless, of course, you have a job like mine).

The subconscious mind is the part that you are not aware of, and yet it is always there, controlling your body. It is responsible for things like blinking your eyes, beating your heart, storing emotions, and creating beliefs. Rather like the operating system of a computer, it runs in the background, and you're not even aware of it – until something goes wrong!

The way the subconscious mind makes decisions is very different from the conscious mind.

First, it is always looking for the fastest, most efficient way to a result. Which is why, if you get scared one time, in future it will simply tell your conscious mind to avoid similar situations.

Second, the subconscious mind works primarily with emotions; it doesn't base its choices on logic. That's why when you're arguing with your significant other, and you get emotional, you stop making sense and contradict yourself. And because the subconscious mind is inherently illogical, trying to use logic to think your way out of a phobia will be either very slow or completely ineffectual. It's like talking Russian to a German: the subconscious and the conscious just don't speak the same language.

So, in order to resolve emotions like fears and phobias, you first have to learn how to speak to the subconscious mind in its own language, which is what I will teach you in this book.

Getting to the Root of the Problem

Half the work in clearing phobias is finding the initial trigger. Sometimes, when we explore a phobia, the trigger is obvious (such as being on a flight when you were eight years old and going through severe turbulence). Other times, the connections aren't that clear or logical. Phobias, after all, are a feeling not a statistic, and you create those phobias—that association between a stimulus and a feeling—as a survival strategy.

To make things worse, the cause of a phobia isn't always directly connected to the shock or fear that created it. If, at the exact moment that you were terrified, you happened to see something quite benign –like a coin, say – that coin can become the trigger for feelings of shock or fear in the future, even though it wasn't what caused the fear in the first place

When Claire, a client, first got in touch, she told me she had visited various therapists and tried many techniques and courses to try to overcome her fear of planes, but none of them had helped. As we talked, I realised that all those other therapists had focused on the aircraft. They would say things like, "Think about the plane, look around and notice how safe it is." or "Relax. Notice how calm you can feel when on a plane." What they had missed was that in Claire's case, although it was a plane that triggered the phobia, the actual association was with something completely different.

With Claire, what those well-meaning therapists had failed to explore was what was going on around her at the time her fear of planes started. We discovered that she'd been involved in a traumatic event, and as she was fleeing the area to try and get away, she had caught a plane. She sat on the flight reliving what happened over and over, trying to make sense of the situation. Now, whenever Claire looked at an aircraft, she was reliving the traumatic memory of that flight. Claire wasn't aware of any of this logically. Her conscious mind had no understanding of the connections her brain was making; she was just aware of the feelings of dread and fear that came up every time she had to take a plane somewhere.

Sometimes you need to look beyond the obvious trigger and understand that the subconscious mind doesn't always work in the same way as our conscious mind.

First, you have to remember that sometimes the causes of a phobia can seem irrelevant when we look back. That's because an experience that an adult would find trivial, if they even noticed it, can seem huge – out of all proportion – if it happens to a child.

Second, because of how your subconscious mind works, even if two people have similar experiences, the meaning they derive from those events – the beliefs, feelings, or even fears and phobias their subconscious mind stores away for future decision making – can be very different.

Triggers from the past

To make things even more interesting when we're looking for triggers, the subconscious mind can play some interesting tricks on us when it's trying to process an experience. Specifically, there are three ways that our subconscious mind makes things seem different: deletion, distortion, and generalisation.

Deletion is a mechanism that is actually designed to protect us from overwhelm. The brain receives a lot more information than it can process. So, your subconscious mind decides what is most useful to focus on, and what to discard.

> Let me give you an example.
>
> Look around the room you are in and count how many red items there are. Look really carefully, and make sure you examine every object, so you know exactly how many red items there are. Then come back here for the next part of the exercise. Away you go.
>
> OK. If you're back, then I assume you went away and counted all the red items. Now, without looking up or recounting, I want you to write down how many *blue* items there are in the room.
>
> You have no idea, do you? That's because while you were focusing on counting red objects, your subconscious mind ignored all the blue objects. They weren't relevant to the task in hand. That's deletion at work. In a similar way, your subconscious mind will delete things that contradict your beliefs. It does that so that you won't get distracted at a critical moment rethinking past decisions.

Now, what does that have to do with your fear of flying? Remember, the subconscious mind wants to get to the result quickly. If it has decided that flying is dangerous, the last thing it needs is to be weighing up contradictory evidence that would just confuse the issue. So, if you believe flying is unsafe, you'll ignore the facts that thousands of flights happen every day without incident, but you'll latch onto an air accident on the news, even if it happened thousands of miles away.

Distortion works similarly—and for similar reasons—but instead of ignoring inconvenient facts, your subconscious mind looks for an interpretation that fits your existing beliefs. If you've ever told someone something and then later you found out that they heard what they wanted to hear (usually the exact opposite of what you actually said), that was their subconscious mind distorting what they heard to match their expectations. When we're looking for the meaning of an event, distortion leads us to draw the wrong conclusions and therefore learn the wrong lesson.

So, you're sitting at the gate waiting to board and you see the crew go past laughing, but the pilot is looking down seriously at his notes. In your mind, you've already decided he's seen something worrying about the plane or the weather or whatever, whereas in fact, the sheet of paper was a message from his car mechanic to let him know that the new paint job is going to be more expensive than they discussed.

Finally, **Generalisation** is a process that's designed to help us learn. The brain uses generalisation to discover how the world works from specific examples. It's how you learned as a child, for instance, that a flat surface with four legs and a back was a chair. It's also how you learned not to touch hot surfaces: because one day you put your hand on a hot stove and burned yourself. So, we take an experience and draw general conclusions from it.

When it works, it's useful. However, sometimes we draw the wrong conclusions, or we over-generalise. The Little Albert experiment I mentioned above didn't stop with the rat. Once Watson and his assistant had made Albert thoroughly terrified of white rats, they started to introduce other "stimuli": a white rabbit, a furry dog, a seal-skin coat, even a Santa Claus mask with a white cotton wool beard. Each time, Albert got distressed and started to cry, just like he had with the rat. In other words, he'd generalised his fear of the rat to other furry objects.

Generalisation is one of the main ways that people with a flying phobia support their fear. If they hear about a fault with a plane, it becomes "every plane has faults", if there's a story in the news about a drunk pilot, it becomes "every pilot is an alcoholic", and of course, every report of a plane crash becomes proof that all planes are unsafe.

In one of my workshops, an audience member shared that even though her fear of flying had started with a specific event, she had recently noticed herself feeling afraid on other means of transport like boats and trains. She'd started with some event that made her subconscious mind think "Flying is dangerous", then over time that had been generalised into "travel is dangerous."

It's All a Big Misunderstanding

As you can probably guess from what I've just described, your phobia is actually a misunderstanding on the part of your subconscious mind that tricks your brain into believing danger is present when it isn't. The fastest, most effective and lasting way to overcome phobias, as we'll see later in this book, is to retrain your brain to remove the overactive 'danger' response.

If you search on YouTube for "7-minute flying phobia cure" you'll find a video of me working with, Louise, a client who'd had a fear of flying for twenty years. I tracked her phobia back to the first time that she ever felt this fear. She remembered her parents getting agitated and anxious about a flight when she was a child. They weren't scared, they were just rushing to get everything ready, making sure they had all the addresses they needed and the travel details, and they just wanted to be on holiday not waiting at the airport.

All those things seem minor to an adult, but to the small child Louise, it was enough for her mind to think, "flying is dangerous." Unknowingly, her subconscious had held onto that belief as she grew older, so she had always looked at planes as something to be fearful of. Once Louise realised this and could look back from an adult perspective, it was easy to change that belief and completely let go of the fear. Now, Louise cannot wait to go travelling and get on a plane, and she says that, if she had the money, she would be going on holiday every week.

> You can watch the original session and a follow-up video Louise recorded 3 years later, here:
>
> www.FaceYourFearOfFlying.com

Anxiety: the fear of fear itself

There's another aspect of fear that is harder to deal with (though we will deal with it in this book!): anxiety. If you have tried many different ways to get over your phobia and it hasn't changed, that could be because it's anxiety-based. With an anxiety-based phobia, there isn't one single event that made your brain think, *Oh, this is dangerous*, but rather a series of experiences over time.

For example, imagine someone going through a turbulent period in their family life: a divorce, having a very anxious or aggressive parent, being bullied at school, or having long-term stress at work. Because there's a lot going on rather than a single big event, the subconscious mind can't link one specific thing (such as dogs, flying, or public speaking) to danger. Instead, it perceives the whole world as dangerous.

That creates thoughts like *I can't cope,* or *I'm not safe,* and soon your Fight, Flight, or Freeze response triggers in an attempt to protect you every time you're outside your comfort zone.

Anxiety is like having lots of phobias running at the same time. You might think they are separate, but they all derive from a core belief that you're not safe or that you need to be on your guard. Until you've cleared those thoughts and feelings—until you feel secure within yourself—then it's hard to change your feelings of anxiety. Some of the self-soothing exercises in this book can help.

Another area that often requires work if your fear of flying is anxiety-based is the fear of the future. Anxiety creates a stream of *what-ifs*: "What if I'm not safe?" "What if I'm not protected?" "What if my fear comes back?" Ironically, of course, these are all fears of fear itself: you're imagining yourself in the future and worrying that you might not be able to cope with your emotions. If you had a panic attack in the past, you fear that you might have a panic attack in the future, that you might embarrass yourself, or that you'll be so overwhelmed you can't cope. So, in an attempt to protect you, your mind tries to make you avoid those things.

Fear is a feeling, but anxiety is something you *do*. The more you worry about the fact that you might worry, the more worry you create. And then you say to yourself, *See? I was right to worry!* It becomes a self-fulfilling prophecy and the fear spirals.

Now that you understand how fear can lead to a phobia, it puts you in a position of power. The next time something makes you feel scared, rather than letting it turn into a phobia you can get to work on it quickly and avoid having to live a life where you have to avoid that trigger.

What you resist, persists

When you fight a feeling, it can come back stronger. You see this all the time when you argue with someone: you have your opinion, they have a completely different one, and as each of you resists the other's point of view, the argument escalates but goes nowhere. And yet, another time, you're not in the mood to argue, so you just say "Yes, sure" and you let the other person's opinions go over your head. How quickly does that person run out of steam? The argument just falls flat very quickly.

It's the same with your emotions, especially your fear, phobia, or anxiety. That's why, when you fight your phobia, and you tell yourself "I just don't want to feel these feelings," and try to push them down, they pop back up stronger and bigger. Instead, the next time you get scared, fearful, anxious, or phobic, do this. Sit with the feeling and notice everything about it. Sometimes, you'll find that simply being in the moment can cause that emotion to disappear. For some people, this happens quite quickly. For others it may take a few minutes. Either way, it's OK.

If YOU have a phobia and you would like to dig deep and work on it so that you can move from fear to freedom, book a clarity call with me and let's chat about how I can set you free from your phobia.

www.ChristopherPaulJones.com/free-clarity-call

CHAPTER THREE

Introducing The Integrated Change System

There are many different systems for creating change. Each of them deals better with some aspects of human thought and behaviour than the others, and all of them have their own strengths and weaknesses. In this chapter, I discuss a number of these alternative approaches before presenting the system that I created myself based on my experience of healing my own phobia and working with thousands of clients to clear theirs: The Integrated Change System™.

You can approach removing a flying phobia from several different directions. The specific areas treatment needs to address are:

- Your **thoughts and beliefs** on the subject of flying.
- The **images** you create in your mind about flying.
- Your **feelings** and emotions when you think about flying.
- The **automatic** (Pavlovian) **responses** you experience as part of your phobia.
- The emotional events in your **history** that contributed to how the phobia was created.   The techniques and systems for creating change we discuss in this chapter often focus on just one or two of these and ignore the rest. Unfortunately, that usually means the treatment only addresses part of the problem, making it less effective.

Individual Approaches to Phobias

I am trained in all the techniques you'll read about below, and while I am not against any of these methods themselves, most of them fall short when they're used on their own because, as I said above, their focus is too narrow. I created the Integrated Change System to address the shortcomings of individual modalities by taking the best from each approach, using the strengths of each one to overcome the shortcomings of the others.

Cognitive Behavioural Therapy

Cognitive Behavioural Therapy (CBT) focuses mainly on becoming aware of automatic or catastrophic **thoughts** (like *What if it all goes wrong?*). CBT primarily deals with phobias by exposing the person to their fear.

The objective is to learn to cope with your fear rather than eliminating it, potentially turning every day into an emotional battle with your fear. This can be a painful process and, in many cases, can make the client feel worse!

While CBT doesn't pay much attention to the feelings, the history, or the subconscious triggers that created the phobia, it does have some useful tools for focusing on the issue and making you more aware of your thoughts. But even at its best, it tends to teach you how to cope with your fears rather than how to transform and change them.

The Integrated Change System aims instead to remove the triggers so that you no longer feel emotional about your old fear, phobia or anxiety. With the approach you learn in this book, you will not need to face your fear until you are ready and you no longer have any emotion about it.

Counselling

Counselling encourages you to explore your feelings by talking and having the therapist reflect back to you from time to time. While talking through your problem can be helpful because you feel heard and you gain self-understanding about why you have a phobia, understanding alone rarely creates any kind of long-term change. Counselling can also be a lengthy process, and you may have to wait a long time before you see any difference.

Hypnotherapy

Hypnotherapy aims to change your **thoughts** and **feelings** about your phobia. A significant strength of hypnotherapy in treating phobias is that it's not a "talking" therapy. Instead, hypnotherapy taps directly into the subconscious which – as we saw in Chapter Two – plays a major role in creating and maintaining your phobia.

The downside with many types of hypnotherapy is that unless you deal first with the root causes of your fear of flying, it either won't work or the fear will come back after a short time. However, working on the subconscious mind directly makes hypnotherapy a very powerful way to create change once those underlying causes have been addressed.

Informational events and seminars

You'll often see "get over your fear of flying events" advertised by airlines or individual pilots. These are typically built around the kind of facts and statistics about flight safety you saw in Chapter One: in other words, they're trying to change your phobia with lots of information.

If your phobia really is based on a simple misunderstanding of the level of risk, then facts and figures may be enough to help you change. Otherwise, we've already seen why a purely analytical approach to treating a phobia is unlikely to be effective.

I designed the Integrated Change System to work on the emotional components of your fears, rather than just giving information.

Pills or drinking

Some phobia sufferers try to deal with their phobia by drinking themselves into a stupor or taking other substances (legal or otherwise) to block their **automatic responses** and catastrophic **thoughts** until it's all over. This is, at best, a short-term solution and also carries the risk of severe and unpleasant side effects.

Of course, that's not to say medication is not sometimes necessary. If you have a prescription from your doctor, it can be helpful as a short-term solution to get you through a specific trip. But, in the long term, it would be better to deal with the root of the issue so you won't need to rely on pills.

Mindfulness/Yoga

Many people turn to techniques like yoga and tai chi, which use physical movement to help you feel calm and centred, or contemplative techniques like meditation and mindfulness. These are useful daily practises for staying balanced and being present. However, they don't deal with the root causes of your phobia or your fears of the future.

Rapid change processes

Rapid change methods like NLP, EMDR, tapping (EFT/TFT), etc. are different from the approaches above in that they can deal with the past quickly and effectively, and when they do work the results can be amazing. I use many tools from these techniques in the Integrated Change System to great effect.

However, many practitioners of these methods, especially those trained in short courses, don't understand how the tools work and, therefore, what to do when they don't. For example, they might work on something in the client's past but not realise that they need to deal with the fear of the future.

What do you choose?

So, when it comes to your phobia, what's the "best" way to deal with it? As you've probably guessed, the answer is that none of the techniques above is best on its own, although they can each have a place in helping you deal with your phobia.

Many of the techniques attempt to deal with the cause of your phobia by making you relive the negative experience that created it. However, neuroscientists have discovered that if you relive a negative experience from your past without doing anything to change the emotions and responses that went with it, you often end up reinforcing the negative feelings rather than releasing them. So, you can end up making your phobia worse.

Often, clients come to me after they've already tried one way of treating their phobia and either failed or had limited results. For example, they may have dealt with their thoughts, but not their feelings. So, they've gone from not even being able to go near a plane to being able to sit in one but shaking all through the flight.

It's an improvement, but the fear is still there because the therapy only addressed a single aspect of the phobia. Treatment needs to work on all aspects of how your phobia was created, which is why I developed the Integrated Change System: to explore your fear from all directions and ensure you get the fullest and most complete change.

Putting Them All Together

The aim of the Integrated Change System is for you to no longer have the symptoms at all. It's not about coping or having to put all your energy into just "getting by", but rather permanently changing your emotional response so that when you see the thing you used to fear, you no longer experience a reaction.

The Integrated Change System incorporates aspects of many of the methods I described above. Over the years, I've been certified to the highest levels in many of them—even to the point of being able to train and certify others myself—which provided me with an opportunity to observe many practitioners, and what I noticed is that they typically make two mistakes.

First, they try to tackle the issue without understanding it. For example, if a client says they have a fear of flying, the practitioner focuses on that. However, flying might not be the real underlying fear. We'll see later in the book that flying phobia can often, for example, stem from other fears such as fear of heights or of not being in control

Second, practitioners often fail to understand that a phobia is trying to meet a subconscious need—albeit a destructive or illogical one. It's a little like having an ugly beam in your brand-new house that blocks your view. You could go ahead and tear it down, but what if it turns out it's doing a useful job like supporting the floor above? We'll see later in the book that sometimes your subconscious mind sets up a phobia because it thinks it's helping you and keeping you safe and protected by making you avoid your fear trigger. If a practitioner removes the phobia without ensuring the underlying need is met, the mind will try to find some other way to fulfil that need – a bit like someone who quits smoking but ends up overeating instead because the tobacco was really a way to meet an emotional need.

Why Are You Reading This Book?

Too often, when people think about their phobia of flying, they think about what they *don't* want – "I don't want to feel bad," "I don't want to feel scared," etc. – rather than on what they *do* want. Unfortunately, in order to process a negative, the subconscious mind first has to think about the thing it's trying to cancel out.

For example, if I say to you *don't think of a blue tree with blue leaves blowing in the wind*, you probably immediately think of a blue tree with blue leaves blowing in the wind. Then, you start to change it by, for example, making the leaves red or green. You may have tried out a few different looks before settling on one. You may even have felt a twinge of anxiety as you tried to figure out what the "right" answer was, and whether you should just obliterate the tree altogether. However you got there, the point is that you had to start by thinking of the blue tree first, which means you began by focusing on what you don't want.

If instead, I say *Think of a red tree with golden leaves dropping gently to the ground*, your mind can go straight there. There's no wondering what you should be thinking about and whether you got it "right". Focusing on what you do want rather than what you don't want makes a massive difference in our neurology. In the same way, focusing on how you want to feel rather than how you *don't* want to feel will make a massive difference in how you feel about your fear of flying.

So, before we go through the seven steps of the Integrated Change System, it's important for you to find out what you want to achieve from reading this book.

- What's your outcome for reading this book? What is it you want to get, do, be, or have by being phobia free?
- What will that give you?
- How will you know when you have it? What will you hear, see, and feel when you have it?

Part Two

Seven Action Steps to Break Through Your Flying Phobia

In this part of the book, you'll learn a systematic approach to help you overcome your flying phobia. Some of the techniques and strategies we use can be done consciously, with your eyes open. Others require you to close your eyes, which I realise is difficult while you're reading a book(!) In the text I'll show you how to access recordings of the techniques to make it easier.

CHAPTER FOUR

Action Step 1: Relax the Conscious Mind and Body

As we've seen, phobias are rooted in emotion. However, because emotions aren't logical, you can't think your way out of the problem. Trying to intellectualise the causes of your phobia consciously doesn't work—indeed, when it comes to dealing with emotions, the conscious mind can get in the way. In the first step of the Integrated Change System, therefore, we relax the conscious mind.

Your physiology has a major influence on how you feel. Don't believe me? Try this simple experiment.

> Focus for a moment on the thing that makes you scared, fearful or anxious.
>
> As you focus on it, notice what happens to your body: Where do your eyes go? What happens to your breathing? To your shoulders? Where is your head?
>
> Shake it out.
>
> Now stick your chest right out, put your head back and your arms down but out to the sides and put the biggest smile you can manage on your face.
>
> While you are doing that—without moving a single muscle—try to focus on that thing you are scared or phobic of.

In this position, you'll find it very difficult to focus on the object of your fears. Why? Because this physiology—this way of holding your body—is incompatible with sadness. Which means that the secret to feeling good is surprisingly simple: all you need to do is change your body language; change how you're moving.

When you have a strong belief about something – for example "flying is dangerous" – you act as though it's true. More importantly, your body reacts like it is true, even though it isn't.

Remember the reptilian brain? If you believe "flying is dangerous", your reptilian brain will trigger the Fight, Flight or Freeze response: you break out into a cold sweat, your heart starts to race, you begin to breathe faster, and of course you may feel an urgent need to go to the loo.

So, now you're not just thinking about your fear, you're feeling afraid, and your body is acting as though you're in real danger.

Then, the rest of your body goes along with it. Some people try to curl up defensively, others grip the armrest so hard their knuckles turn white – or they grip their partner so hard it hurts.

And then – and here is where your brain is just messing with you – the mammalian brain and the neocortex notice what your body is doing, and you unconsciously think "those are my danger signals. I must be in danger!" and the whole thing spirals.

Which is interesting.

Because, if having the physiology of fear is a signal to your brain to be afraid, it means we can start to break that spiral in a very simple way: simply by adopting a calm, relaxed physiology.

Learning to Relax by Opening Your Awareness

There are many relaxation techniques that can help you to still your mind, such as mindful meditation. In this book, however, we will achieve it through what we call "open" or "wide awareness".

The particular technique you're about to learn has been used for thousands of years and is one of the pillars of the Hawaiian practice called Huna.

Although the exercise is done with your eyes open, you won't be able to look at the book as you do it, so read through the instructions several times to familiarise yourself with the steps, then try it out.

1. Stand up straight, with your feet shoulder-width apart.
2. Smile!
3. Stretch both arms out in front of you and touch your index fingers together.
4. Choose a spot on the wall just above eye level (sometimes, it can help focus if you put a mark on the wall where you will be looking, or choose a fixed object such as a clock).
5. Keeping your eyes fixed on the spot you selected, slowly move your fingers apart, keeping your arms at shoulder level
6. Stretching your arms out to the sides, and looking straight ahead at the spot on the wall all the time, use your peripheral vision to keep both fingers in view at all times—you should find you also start to see more detail of what is around you. NOTE: This exercise involves eye muscles that most people don't use often, so you may find that it makes your eyes water. Keep practising and it will pass.

7. Keeping your view wide, let your arms drop to the sides. That view is called open or wide awareness.
8. Take a deep breath in and out as you hold that peripheral vision. Notice that when you keep that raised awareness and stay focused, a lot of the internal chatter and self-talk will start to quieten down and dissipate.
9. Relax and return to normal vision.

How do you feel?

When we use open awareness, it turns off a lot of the mind chatter, which also allows you to take in more information and reduce distractions.

Body Scanning

Now that your mind is at rest, let's help you to relax physically too. Body scanning is a technique that isolates and relaxes groups of muscles in turn. It works so well that it's often used in hypnosis recordings and self-hypnosis. In the course of the exercise, you're going to close your

Action Step 1: Relax the Conscious Mind and Body [47]

eyes, so read through it several times until you're clear about what you are going to do.

> 1. Rest your feet loosely on the ground and put your hands on your lap.
> 2. Take a slow deep breath in through your nose and out through your mouth.
> 3. Breathe in as you slowly and silently count to 5 in your mind, "1...2...3...4...5...", and then breathe out as you again slowly count in your mind, "1...2...3...4...5..."
> 4. Imagine a big, bright golden light circulating above the top of your head. Now, allow that light to start to scan your body, as that spinning light comes down through the top of your head, filling you up with a warm light that's so relaxing.

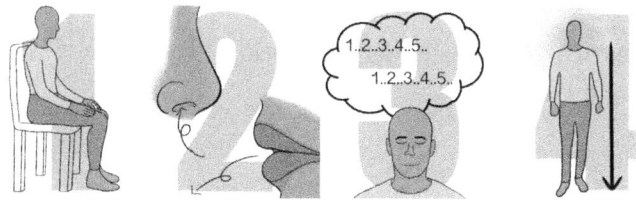

> 5. Let the light come down to your eyebrows, allowing all tension in your body to just disappear. If you're holding any tension in the top of your head, just let it drain away. And then let it go past your eyes and allow your eyes to relax. Look at the back of your eyelids.
> 6. As that bright light fills you up, let it come down to your jaw and allow your jaw to relax

7. As you take another deep breath in, and connect to that part of you that beats your heart, blinks your eyes, and stores all your emotions
8. Just allow the light to come into your throat and then down into your shoulders.

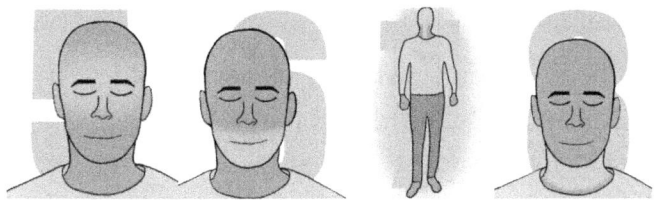

9. Relaxing the muscles, allow yourself to breathe effortlessly and just let the light come into your chest, filling up your heart with this bright golden light. And allow yourself to relax.
10. If there's any tension in your body, shake it out, and breathe the light into you.
11. Then come down into your legs, into your knees, finally filling your feet up so you're completely grounded
12. As you take another deep cleansing breath, just open your eyes and come back to now.

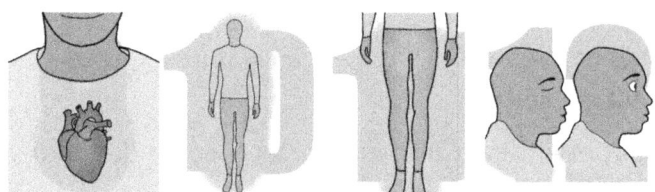

Take a moment again to notice how you feel. If you've done the exercise properly, you'll be wonderfully relaxed throughout your body. And when you're totally relaxed, you're ready for the next step.

FREE RESOURCE

Many of the exercises in this book can be hard to follow in print. That's why I wanted to make it easier for you!

You can download a FREE audio recording of this exercise and others from the book at:

www.FaceYourFearOfFlying.com

CHAPTER FIVE

Action Step 2: Get Precision

Nobody likes feeling fearful or uncertain, and in order for us to get from there into a place of feeling certain and confident, we need a step in the middle. As we've seen in earlier chapters, the fear and uncertainty you feel when your phobia is triggered are caused by a pattern—a series of steps like a computer program—that starts to run in your brain and creates the fear. So, if you want to feel something other than fear, we need to scramble that fear pattern.

Emotions are scary things for many people, and it's logical to try to keep yourself safe by staying in your conscious mind a lot of the time, which can make you overly analytical. The underlying idea is that if you can just make sense of the world, you'll be safe. But that approach isn't going to help you get to the root of what's causing you to be afraid, because, as we've seen, fear isn't built on logical, rational reasons.

> The whole process was eye-opening, and finally understanding where my phobia comes from has been a huge help in trying to control it.
> **Morgane Le Caer – PopSugar Magazine**

Ours Not to Reason Why

When you're trying to overcome flying phobia, it's tempting to ask yourself questions like "Why am I afraid of flying?" The problem is that asking why something is happening just encourages you to list all your fears and concerns, so it tends to keep you stuck in the problem.

When I'm working with clients, I'll ask them, "When did this fear start?" Usually, there's a long silence before they say they don't know. When I point out it was a long silence just to get to "I don't know," the response is almost always something along the lines of "Well, I thought of a bunch of things. But they don't make sense, so they can't be right."

In fact, what many people really mean when they say, "I don't know," is "I've thought of a reason, but it doesn't make sense, so I'll ignore it."

To get the right answer, you need to get out of your own way and connect to your subconscious. As you work through the questions below, notice all the answers your mind gives you, and pay attention to them. Because it is in those answers that you will find solutions.

Getting Clear

In this section, we're going to get to the core of your fear by understanding what you're *really* afraid of and when you first *created* it.

"Fear of flying" can mean many things, from "I get a little nervous going through check-in, but then I have a beer and I feel fine," through to "If anyone so much as mentions flying, I curl up on the floor in a foetal position," and everything in between. You could also look at two people who have "fear of flying" and find that they are actually afraid of different aspects of flying, such as

- Heights
- Turbulence/movement
- Being confined and not being able to get off the plane
- Not being in control
- Falling
- Being scared or embarrassing yourself

And these aren't mutually exclusive: your fear of flying might actually be made up of several of these fears, not just one. Sometimes you can see a direct link between that fear and a fear of flying, but sometimes the connection is less obvious. In the table below, you'll see some examples of the kind of thing that can trigger a fear of flying. As you read them, you may find yourself thinking of how your own fear came into being. Even if nothing comes to mind immediately, don't worry: later in the book, we'll use other techniques that delve deeper into your subconscious to bring up and resolve past triggers.

Fear	Example direct link	Example indirect link
Heights	You were on a plane and something happened that made you afraid.	You were taken up a tall building as a child and felt afraid.
Turbulence	You were on a bumpy flight in the past.	You were on a scary theme park ride
Being confined or unable to get off	You felt trapped on a flight between the 'plus-sized' passenger in the seat next to you and the passenger in front who tipped their seat back.	As a child you got stuck in a lift or a cupboard. Or you had a very strict parent, and you weren't allowed out of the house
Not being in control	You got emotional on a plane and felt you were not in control of your own feelings.	Growing up, you felt you had very little freedom because your parents controlled everything. Or you were a passenger in a car that crashed when someone else was driving.

Falling or crashing	Watching a plane crash on the news or in a movie.	You fell off a swing and got hurt as a child. You were in a highly emotional state, and you watched a car crash on a TV show.
Fear of being scared (fear of the fear)	You had a panic attack (possibly caused by something completely different) while you were on a plane.	You had stage fright before going on stage in the school play, and when you went on, you made a fool of yourself. Or you were going through a prolonged period of stress at work or home.

You can probably see that events that are directly linked to fear of flying are much easier to identify when you're trying to think of the root cause of your fear. But when the link is less direct (like losing a parent when you were a child), it can be harder. In fact, you might even remember the event but think to yourself, "Oh, but it can't be that. That has *nothing* to do with flying."

What am I afraid of?

The first step to getting clarity is to ask yourself: What is it specifically that I'm afraid of when it comes to flying?

> Grab a pen and paper and answer that for yourself right now:
> - What specifically am I afraid of when it comes to flying? What am I focusing on when my fear kicks in?

A good way to figure this out is ask **When is my fear at its worst?** For example:

- When the plane is climbing (often connected to a fear of not being in control).
- When the plane levels out at cruising altitude, and you can look out of the windows (in which case, you probably have a phobia of heights rather than flying).
- The moment the door shuts, and you can't get out? (in which case, your fear is probably something closer to claustrophobia).
- If there is turbulence on the flight (then you may be afraid of the movement, or you're imagining dropping out of the sky).
- What if I panic on the plane? (If so, you have a fear of the fear; a fear of not being in control of your emotions).

Later in this book, when we come to the change methods, I use the term "fear of flying". If you have realised that your issue is really about something else – control, heights, or whatever – you can change the wording in your mind as you read this book.

When did it start?

The next step in creating change is to find out what caused your fear in the first place. This is something I spend a lot of time on with my one-on-one clients, using relaxation and hypnotic techniques to tap into the subconscious mind. For now, we are going to work out consciously when your fear was created.

If you have a fear of heights, for example, when did you first create that fear of being high up? You might think it was when you looked out of a plane window, realised how high up you were, and got scared. But it could just as easily have been when you were 4 years old, stood on a high building, looked down, and felt frightened.

A client once told me he'd been afraid of heights for 12 years, but he'd only been afraid of flying for 7 years. For the first five years, he'd been scared of heights, but he'd been OK with flying. Then one day he was on a plane feeling anxious about something else, and he looked out of the window and thought "Gosh, I'm really up high." In that moment, the two fears became linked in his neurology.

But I'm afraid of so many things?

In many ways, a phobia is like those games where there's a tower of wooden bricks, and you have to pull the bricks out one at a time until the whole tower falls. When you find the right fear and clear it, you'll find the rest crumble away without much extra work. But, how do you know which one to focus on if your fear of flying is a composite of many different fears? How do you know which one you need to clear to make the others disappear?

Simple: you start with the most significant and work backwards. If you clear that one and the others are still there, work on the next most significant, and keep doing that until you feel better.

Finding Your Triggers

As well as understanding how your phobia started, it's also critical to understand what situations trigger your phobia now, since that can give us valuable information about where to focus.

Jennifer, a dancer, came to me for help with her fear of flying. As I dug a little deeper, it emerged that she was only really afraid of flying over water, and as we continued to work together, she realised that it wasn't flying she was afraid of, it was water! When she was little, her father had tried to teach her to swim, but he had been pushy and authoritarian, which did not work for a young girl who needed more emotional support. His approach had instilled in her a fear of water which her subconscious later generalised to a fear of flying over water.

If I had simply asked her to logically think about where her fear came from, she would never have made the connection between flying and her childhood swimming lessons.

The Flying Phobia Questionnaire

Use this questionnaire to capture the details of your fearful thoughts that lead to your phobic response. Answer the questions as honestly as you can. Even if the answer doesn't make any logical sense, stick with your initial reaction rather than sugar-coating the answer, because that is the most powerful.

1. When you think of your flying phobia, what specifically are you predicting will happen when you fly? What are some examples of the catastrophes that you are anticipating?
2. How negative (0-100%) is the outcome you are predicting?
3. What makes you think this will happen?
4. How likely (0-100%) is it really that this will happen?
5. How many times have you been wrong in the past about your phobia? What actually happened?
6. When you've predicted catastrophes in the past, have they actually come true for you?
7. What are the pros and cons of holding onto your flying phobia?
8. What evidence do you have from the past that your flying phobia has been HELPFUL to you? (e.g. You didn't have to attend a wedding in another country for a relative you don't like).

9. What evidence do you have from the past that your flying phobia has been HURTFUL to you? (e.g. Because of your phobia, you MISSED a family wedding you wanted to go to).
10. Are you able to give up the need for control in order to be less fearful?
11. Does your fear really give you control, or do you feel more out of control because you have a flying phobia?
12. What could you do differently to lessen your fear of flying?
13. Imagine that your flying phobia no longer exists. How will you feel when the fear is gone?

    - What would you gain?
    - What might you lose?

14. If someone else was facing your flying phobia, would you encourage that person to act like you?
15. What advice would you give him or her to deal with it?
16. If you think of your flying phobia, which of these specific fears sum it up the best:

    - Fear of heights
    - Fear of loss of control
    - Fear of being confined or stuck
    - Fear of turbulence
    - Fear of something else

    What made you choose that answer?

17. Where does this fear come from?

18. When did it start?

    - What are your thoughts about this?
    - Approximately, how old were you?
    - Can you think of a time before this?
    - Did you have a fear of flying then?

19. When you feel your fear of flying, what is your inner voice saying to you? *e.g. "I think we are going to crash, something awful is going to happen."*
20. What is the MOST fearful part of the flight? E.g. Takeoff, landing, customs, etc
21. What is the LEAST fearful part of the flight?
22. What are the differences between the most and the least fearful in terms of:

    - What you are thinking.
    - What you are focusing on.
    - What you are believing.
    - Your breathing.

23. What can you learn from this?
24. What can you do differently on your next flight if you choose to?
25. What have you learned about your fear of flying from doing these questions?

CHAPTER SIX

Action Step 3: Find the Benefit Behind your Phobia

The mind doesn't create problems at random. If you have a phobia, it's because, at some point, your subconscious mind believed it would be useful; that it served a purpose.

I had been working with one of my fear of flying clients, and I had helped him deal with several different issues, but he still could not get on a plane. "I don't have the fear anymore," he told me. "I don't have the anxiety, the fear of heights, or the claustrophobia. I just can't get on the plane and I don't know what the problem is."

As we talked, we discovered that his wife had once said to him, "We are going to travel the world, and once we've done that we will settle down and have a family." The problem was, he liked being young and having freedom. So, in that moment, his brain thought *I'm not ready to have a family*. He'd been holding on to the fear purely because if he let it go, he would be able to travel the world, and when he returned home, he would have to settle down and start a family. His fear kept him from having to step up, have a family, and be an adult; and to his subconscious mind, if he let go of the fear, he would "lose" his freedom.

The Problem was Once the Solution

Milton Erickson was a pioneering hypnotherapist and psychologist in the 1960s. He was the first person to get hypnotherapy recognised as a legitimate therapy by the medical profession.

One of his favourite sayings was "the problem was once the solution." In other words, however destructive a behaviour or pattern may be, there was once a time or a context where it was the best response the mind could find to whatever was going on. Problems arise when that becomes the *only* solution available to you. For example, a nightclub doorman came to see me with anger management issues. I asked him what the benefit might be of having that anger. He explained that in the context of his work, where he was keeping order and controlling whether or not someone can come into the club, it was an entirely appropriate response because he didn't want people to 'mess' with him. However, that pattern of anger had become generalised and spread into other areas of his life where it wasn't an appropriate response, like talking to his boss or interacting with his family.

The same is true of your fear of flying. There will have been a context in your past where being hyper-alert and ready to cope with the situation would have been the best response the mind could give you. It's tempting to want to simply get rid of your fear. However, there may be times when that response is still useful. So, rather than just deleting the problem, sometimes it may be better to allow the subconscious mind to find more options for handling a situation.

When It's Hard to Let Go

I'm always amazed how many clients come to me for help to get over a flying phobia, but then fight me at every turn. Sometimes, I'll get a phone call from someone who says, "I've seen that video where you fixed that lady in seven minutes. I've seen your other stuff, and it seems you know what you're doing. But, you're not going to be able to fix *me* in seven minutes."

The first thing I say to them is, "I'm not fixing anyone; that's not my job. I'm just here to guide you."

The second thing I say is, "I'm not saying it will take seven minutes for everyone. Everyone's mind is different, everyone's causes and reasons for hanging on to it is different. That's why we cover it in the seven steps. But, if it could, why would you *not* want it to take seven minutes?"

And when I question these people, they often say something along the lines of, "If it's so trivial it can be fixed in seven minutes, why have I had it for thirty years?"

That's a slippery slope. It's almost like they're starting to blame themselves for not getting rid of their phobia sooner. That's ridiculous. How can it be their fault when they had no idea it could be fixed, and even if they knew, they didn't have the right tools.

But, it's much easier to live in a world where getting rid of their phobia is hard work, if not impossible, so that the subconscious mind has an excuse to stay as it is.

You Are Not Your Fear

Another reason why clients sometimes fight to hold onto their phobia is when it's become part of who they are. There's a big difference, for example, between someone who says "I've *got* a flying phobia," and someone who says "I *am* afraid of flying." The first implies you have something which therefore you can get rid of if you don't want it. The second is a statement about your identity, your very sense of being. When a client fights me to hold on to their fear, phobia, or anxiety, they are basically saying, "This is part of who I am. I can't separate my own personality from my fear."

You have to realise that your fear is simply an incorrectly learnt pattern—nothing more, nothing less.

Why the Reason For Your Fear Is What's Making It Worse

"The only thing we have to fear is... fear itself.
Franklin Delano Roosevelt.

Although what you're ultimately trying to achieve is to stay safe, there can be many other factors involved. For example, while a phobia is often supported by a secondary gain of safety, there can also be an element of reward.

How can a phobia be a reward? Well, if as a child you were "rewarded" with a hug when you got upset, your mind can associate having problems with receiving love, and you subconsciously hang onto your fear as a way to get the reward. As a result, a pattern that is trying to achieve safety and love at the highest level can be the very thing that ends up blighting your life.

If we take romantic relationships as an example, if one partner feels insecure and is terrified of being left or abandoned, they'll often tell their partner they're not sure they love them. They may accuse them of cheating or ask them where were they at particular times. If that happens over and over again, the other partner will start to feel trapped and mistrusted, and they'll begin to withdraw from the relationship. In this way, the very thing the insecure person was trying to achieve (security in the relationship) ends up costing them the relationship.

To relate that to your fear of flying, if the highest intention for your pattern of anxiety or fear is to stay safe, it is worth asking yourself how safe and protected do you feel when you're sweating or freaking out before a flight. Usually, you'll find that the highest intention has, in fact, created the exact opposite of what you wanted.

> When you're experiencing negative patterns of behaviour such as fear, ask yourself *"What's the positive intention for this behaviour? What does this give me?"*
>
> Take the answer and ask the same questions about that answer.
>
> Repeat the process, asking the questions about the previous answer until you run out of answers.
>
> The final answer is what we call "the highest positive intention".
>
> *For example:*
>
> **- What's the positive intention for fear?**
>
> *- Fear keeps me ready.*
>
> **- What's the positive intention for being ready?**
>
> *- So I feel safe*
>
> **- What's the positive intention for feeling safe?**
>
> *- When I'm safe, I feel happy*

> Once you've established the highest positive intention for your pattern, follow up by asking yourself whether the behaviour is successfully meeting that intention.
>
> *For example, in the sequence above, the question would be "How happy am I when I'm fearful?"*

For some people, even reaching that conscious realisation is enough to let go of their phobia. I was working with a client from the US by web conference, helping her with her flying phobia. As we did this exercise, we uncovered the fact that her phobia was supposed to be protecting her.

"How protected are you when you're having a panic attack on a plane?" I asked her.

"I'm not," she said. And at that moment the answer went in so deep that her phobia was gone.

If you've had the same kind of reaction, and your phobia is gone, congratulations! Our work is done. That said, you should continue working through the rest of this book to consolidate the change.

Why We Cling to Our Problems

This idea that problems have a benefit, as well as a downside, is so vital that it has a name, "secondary gain". When people come to me with anxiety, there's often a very strong secondary gain such as safety: the pattern of fear or anxiety is the only way they know to be alert and ready to deal with danger. Now, this isn't a logical or rational response. So, when someone with a strong belief that their fear is keeping them safe tries a therapy without first working on that subconscious belief, there's a chance it won't work because their subconscious mind will spend the whole time thinking *But how will I be safe?*

Of course, the truth is that fear doesn't keep you safe, except as one possible choice in the moment that the Fight, Flight, or Freeze response is triggered. The reptilian brain isn't intended to be creative or strategic. It doesn't think in shades of grey or nuances. It thinks in terms of right or wrong; good or bad. When you are face-to-face with danger, the reptilian brain has one job: to decide whether to stand your ground, run away, or play dead. And whichever response it picks is only useful *at that exact moment*.

The problem with secondary gain is that your subconscious mind assumes that in letting go of your fear, you are going to lose the benefits provided by the secondary gain, i.e. not believing you'll be safe or protected. But, even if you eliminate your phobia of flying, your survival mechanism is hard-wired and it will always be with you, no matter how much work you do on letting go of fears from the past. And *that's a good thing*. So, if you've tried other therapies and they didn't work, ask yourself these questions:

> What is the belief I am holding on to that keeps the pattern going?
> If my fear of flying were to disappear now, I know what I would gain, but what would I lose?

Many airlines will allow you to ask to speak to the pilot or the crew if you're afraid of flying. But imagine if you went into the cockpit and the pilot was clearly terrified: sweating profusely and gripping the controls to stop their hands trembling. Would you feel like they were more in control? Would you feel safer? Would you be comforted if they told you, "It's OK; I'm only terrified because I need to make sure nothing goes wrong, I need to be on my guard"? The truth is, a pilot is far better prepared to stop things going wrong and avoid danger if they are relaxed and aware.

If part of you still thinks fear or anger protect you, here's an exercise you can do to show you just how much they weaken you instead.

1. Get a partner and stand facing each other.
2. Put your own hands together as if you are about to pray.
3. Ask your partner to hold your wrists.
4. Think of a time when you felt confident, happy, and calm. When you've got that idea firmly in your mind, ask your partner to try to pull your hands apart. You should find that your hands are quite strong and that you can keep them together as your partner pulls.
5. Next, think instead of a time when you felt fearful or anxious. When you have that memory clear in your mind, ask your partner once again to try to separate your hands. This time, you'll probably find that it's much easier for them to pull your hands apart. This has nothing to do with physical weakness. It's just that negative emotions make your body and your immune system weaker and inhibit your ability to think. That's why sportspeople often try to "psych out" their opponents—to make them scared or angry: if they can do that, they've already won half the battle.

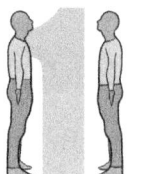  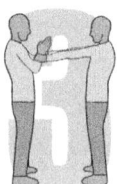 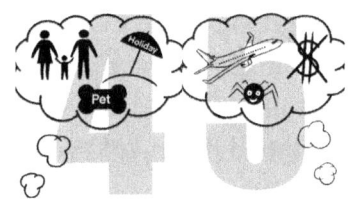

So, your fear doesn't protect you. It keeps you stuck in the reptilian brain and responding like a lizard, not an intelligent, creative thinker with many choices and options. Worse, the more fear you hold on to, the better you become at being afraid, and the less able you are to think logically and rationally about a situation.

Sometimes, however, it's not enough to have a conscious understanding, and we need to tap into your subconscious mind.

> Chris did a few exercises with me to take me into my inner consciousness. At this point, I was feeling a bit cynical. I can only describe them as spatial exercises which involved me focusing on specific objects and sounds as he talked. He then started addressing my inner consciousness, asking it to give him a sign for "yes" and a sign for "no." To my astonishment, I found my body swaying backwards and forwards for "yes" and from side to side for "no." I was still fully aware but in a slight daze.
> **Nikki Garnett – Midlife Chic**

Uncovering the Secondary Gain Unconsciously

One of the easiest ways to uncover the secondary gains from your pattern is to ask your subconscious mind for direct feedback. As you've probably worked out by now, however, the subconscious mind needs simple ways to communicate.

In a moment, I'll guide you through a simple technique called the sway test. It's designed to get a yes/no answer using a mechanism called *biofeedback*—also known as an Ideo-Motor Response (IMR)—which is related to the way you sometimes know instinctively when someone is lying or nervous.

Your subconscious mind is really bad at keeping secrets, and it leaks information all the time through small movements: eye flickers, muscle twitches, etc. Now, most of the time, those movements are so small that they're hard to see. But, if we can make them bigger, then we can see them. So, the sway test is designed to amplify the clues your body is giving.

The curious thing is that, even when you're not consciously aware of the answer to a question, your subconscious knows. It can be quite funny when I'm in session with a client and I ask them something. They'll sit there and say "I don't know" with a perfectly straight face—and they mean it—but meanwhile their foot is waving up and down and their eyelid is flickering so hard it looks like they're trying to wink: that's their subconscious mind trying to tell me that it knows exactly what I asked them for.

Before starting the sway test, it can be helpful to use the relaxation processes in Action Step 1 to get yourself into a calm, relaxed state.

The Yes/No Sway Test

Imagine holding a long ruler in front of you and holding it just at one end. If you make a small movement with your fingers, what happens? The end you're holding hardly moves, but the other end will go up and down quite a lot. In the same way, the sway test uses your whole body to amplify tell-tale little movements that your subconscious mind will make at your ankles.

At one point in the process, I'll ask you to close your eyes. So, just like you did earlier, read through the instructions several times until you've memorized them. As you go through the exercise, make sure you allow your subconscious mind to guide the movements. Don't try to think your way into it or figure out what would "make sense" as a 'yes' or 'no' signal: we are simply asking your subconscious mind to let you know that answer any way it wants to.

How to do it

1. Stand with your feet together and your hands by your side.
2. Expand your awareness so you take in the whole room and you can see to the left and right of you with your peripheral vision without moving your head.
3. Take a deep breath in and allow yourself to relax. Put your head back and close your eyes.
4. Ask your subconscious mind—the part of you that controls all your thoughts, your feelings and your emotions—to give you an involuntary signal for 'yes'. Often, this is a sway forward or back—an involuntary movement that you're not consciously doing or consciously resisting. (For some people it will be a subtle movement, and for others it will be more internal. So, rather than a movement, you might simply feel a sensation like a 'yes' in some part of your body.)
5. Next, ask your subconscious mind to give you a different signal for 'no' and notice where your body moves.
6. Open your eyes

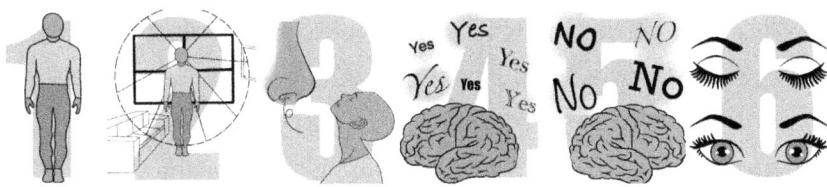

That's how easy it is to talk to your subconscious!

> The oddest, and most effective intervention, however, was when he asked me to stand up and allow my subconscious to indicate to him that it was listening – I was not to do anything consciously. I stood there, feeling rather silly, but gradually felt my body swaying forwards to indicate 'yes', and back for 'no'.
> **Lydia Slater – Deputy Editor, Harper's Bazaar**

Finding the Positive Intent Subconsciously With Yes/No Questions

Now that you've learned how to test yourself with yes/no and true/false questions, let's use that to get to the bottom of why you're struggling to let go of your phobia.

1. Ask your subconscious mind to confirm the signal for 'yes' and a different signal for 'no'.
2. Think about your fear of flying. Ask your subconscious mind "Is there a positive intention for this fear?" and notice when it gives you the signal for "yes".
3. When it's found the positive intention or the need it's trying to meet, just allow that positive intention to come to your conscious awareness.
4. Ask yourself again, "Is there a positive intention for this?" and if your subconscious gives you the signal for "yes", allow the positive intention to come to your conscious awareness.
5. Repeat the process for each new answer, asking if there is a positive intent and, if there is, allowing your subconscious mind to make you aware of it, until you get the answer "no" – when you do, the last answer you got was the highest positive intent.

6. Now ask your subconscious mind whether your fear is the best way to meet that highest positive intent.
7. If it isn't, ask your subconscious mind whether it can find new ways to meet the positive intent in a way that's better for you.
8. And when you're ready, open your eyes.

This is a complex process, especially if you haven't done anything like this before. If you didn't notice a response, or your subconscious mind didn't immediately come up with answers, that's fine. Come back to it and try again.

Want My Guidance?

It can be difficult to work through some of these techniques by reading them in a book, which is why I've recorded all the exercises featured in this book – plus additional tools, techniques, and exercises to help you tackle the most deeply-embedded fears.

In these in-depth recordings, I'll hold your hand and guide you step-by-step as you uncover and deal with the sources of your fear – it's like working with me in person in my Harley Street consulting rooms (but at a fraction of the investment)!

You can find out all about it at

www.FaceYourFearOfFlying.com/virtual

CHAPTER SEVEN

Action Step 4: Uncover the Strategy of your Phobia

A major element of how your phobia develops and progresses is what you put into your mind.

Have you noticed that when you say "I have a fear of flying," people never seem to tell you about all the flights they've been on safely? Instead, they'll go on about the one time that something went wrong. Out of the hundreds of trips they have had, they choose to tell you about the one that was bad.

Of course, it's not just other people who obsess over bad flights. Sometimes, you do it to yourself: I've noticed that many people with a fear of flying also like to watch videos of air crash investigations.

Why do we do that to ourselves?

For some people, there's an underlying hope that if you watch every possible accident, it will somehow give you more control. Imagine if you were about to propose to the love of your life but, before you did, you watched all the YouTube videos you could find of people being rejected when they proposed. How would that help you? It wouldn't. Would you be more in control of your partner's response? Of course not. All it would do is put you into an anxious state.

What you put into your mind has a significant effect on how you feel.

Your internal recipe for feeling afraid

We saw earlier that continually asking yourself *"Why?"* (as in "why is the fear there?") is not a good idea. A better question to ask yourself is *"How?"* How do you 'do' your fear? Because, in order to be afraid, there's a sequence of things you have to do.

If I asked you to teach me how to make a cake, what would you do? First, you would list all the ingredients. Then you would tell me how to put them together in the right order. If I tried to bake a cake, but I left out the eggs, what would happen? It wouldn't work, of course.

What if I did almost everything right, but I waited until I took the cake out of the oven before adding the flour?

What if I was making a chocolate cake, but I left out the chocolate, and instead I put in carrot: I'd have a carrot cake instead of a chocolate cake. I'd have a result, but it would be a different one.

Creating emotions is not too different from making a cake. Your fear, happiness and sadness all have a recipe.

First, to have the pattern of fear, you have to be thinking something like *"This is not safe"*, or *"What if something goes wrong?"* Then, you have to do something to create tension and stress with your feelings, with the self-talk in your head, and with your breathing and posture. Finally, you have to imagine the worst possible outcomes and make big, bright mental images: perhaps you see yourself stuck in your seat, unable to escape, or maybe you see the plane falling from the sky.

Just like baking a cake, however, if you change the recipe, you can change how you feel. If you change the ingredients or the order of the steps, you change the results. How would you feel if you changed how the voice inside your head sounded so that instead of an anxious voice telling you the plane was going to crash, it was a boring voice or a squeaky cartoon voice?

Everything you do has a pattern and a sequence, and the more you can isolate your recipe for fear of flying, the easier it is to work on it and change it. And, just as you have a recipe for creating fear, however, you also have one for happiness. When I'm happy, for example, I make bright images of smiling faces; I feel a tingling in my stomach; and I take deep, relaxed breaths.

Five Questions to Tackle Your Fear of Flying

As we have said, once you have found your recipe for having fear of flying, it becomes easier to know where to focus to change it. So, these questions are designed to help you uncover the recipe.

1. **How do you know when to feel afraid of flying?** What needs to happen for you to be frightened? E.g. somebody says "Let's go on holiday!"
2. **How do you run this pattern?** What is going on in your mind? E.g. "I have to see the plane, then I have to make a vivid image of the plane crashing in my mind."
3. **How do you know that it is fear that you're feeling?** Fear, anxiety, and excitement can all feel very similar. Often, after I've worked with a client, if I ask them to imagine they are on a flight, they might say something like "I'm feeling some anxiety, but it's not the same as it was before." Sometimes if I probe deeper, they say, "Oh it's not anxiety. It's excitement!" So, what's the difference in your mind between anxiety and excitement?

4. **How did you first create this fear pattern?** Where were you at the time? What were you thinking and feeling then?
5. **When did you first create this fear pattern?** What was happening at that time?

TIP: If you find yourself saying "I don't know..." in response to these questions, try to think of four or five events in the past that may have led to your fear of flying.

What Harry Potter Can Teach You About Phobias

In the Harry Potter books and films, J. K. Rowling describes a magical process called the *riddikulus* spell. If you haven't seen the movies or read the books, the *riddikulus* spell takes something you're terrified of and turns it into something humorous instead. For example, one of the young wizards casts *riddikulus* on a spider and suddenly it's on roller skates and it's comical. Another wizard casts the spell on Professor Snape, the scary teacher they don't like, and suddenly he's dressed like an elderly Victorian lady, complete with a parasol and a hat with a dead bird.

Imagine that thing you're scared of when flying. What are you seeing when you think of it? Notice what picture you have in your mind. Also, notice what the soundtrack is. Often, it is the sounds that are going on around you—for example, with a fear of the flight it might be the noise of the engines—or it could be your internal dialogue, your inner voice, saying something like "oh no I'm not safe" in a big loud voice.

What would happen if you were to take those images and that soundtrack and cast the *riddikulus* spell? How would that change your perception in your mind? What if you took your fear of flying and turned it into a Simpsons cartoon in your mind? It would probably reduce the fear.

Then you could take that internal voice, speed it up like we did above, and make it high-pitched and squeaky like a chipmunk.

Or, you could switch the soundtrack altogether and just add in some funny music. For example, when I was young, my dad used to watch an old comedy show on TV called The Benny Hill Show. Every week the show ended with a zany chase scene with the same funny music (it's called "Yakkety Sax" – you can Google it if you want a reminder). Even now, people of all ages know that tune and associate it with laughter. Alternatively, you probably know the tune that is traditionally played at almost every circus when the clowns come on: "Entry of the Gladiators".

Now imagine some aspect of flying that still scares you (for example, takeoff). If you think of that while playing Yakkety Sax or the clown tune in your head, how does that change how you feel?

These kinds of changes remove the emotional charge because it's very hard to have two contrary emotions running at the same time. So, if you're laughing, it's difficult to feel afraid. And that's really how Harry Potter's magical *riddikulus* therapy works.

> I had never expected to be told to imagine my 'anxiety voice' as that of Donald Duck – and I absolutely loved it. I agree wholeheartedly with Chris's notion that you can't be afraid of the ridiculous. Making your fears ludicrous and laughable really does help to get rid of them. In fact, the whole approach of throwing humour at a problem to make it go away was one which hugely appealed to me, and I was overjoyed to find a professional who supported and embraced my own way of looking at my anxieties with an element of entertainment.
> **Jackie John – Mums & Dads Magazine**

> You can watch me doing this process with a client at one of my live events by reconditioning them to thinking their fear of flying is funny.
>
> Watch the full video at www.FaceYourFearOfFlying.com

Time to Scramble Your Recipe

Now that we understand the power of playing with the elements of a fear recipe, and we've identified the ingredients and steps in your own personal recipe, in the rest of this chapter we're going to start changing it and generating a different outcome.

The ingredients of a recipe for fear are typically:

- Beliefs
- Mental imagery
- Self-talk
- Posture
- Breathing
- Triggers

Beliefs

Beliefs can be so powerful that people will fight wars over them. Human history is one long line of conflicts between religious groups, political movements, and ideologies.

Just because people will do a lot in the name of their beliefs, however, doesn't make them real. That's why two people can have completely different beliefs about how the world works.

Where beliefs come from

Your beliefs are normally formed before the age of seven, and regardless of what age you are now, it's likely you still have some of the same beliefs that you acquired as a child. Many of those beliefs came, not surprisingly, from your parents and other people around you. So, it's useful with any belief to ask whose belief it actually is. Is it yours, or did you learn it from watching or listening to someone else?

When I was being filmed for the BBC documentary series *Skies Above Britain*, I was talking to the director about what I did. When I started to describe how we create our beliefs, he told me about a stunt pilot they had interviewed for another episode. The pilot had described how, as a child, he had been taken up in an aeroplane for the first time. He said it was the freest he had ever felt and from that day forward he knew he wanted to be a pilot.

The interesting thing is, if he'd been feeling stressed that day because of something else that was happening—maybe a test he'd failed at school, or a sibling pulling his leg—and he'd felt trapped as he took off, he might instead have made a lifetime choice to never fly again.

The beliefs we create in our early life, if strong enough, can shape our entire future—both good and bad. And with that in mind, it's time to explore what beliefs are holding you back from flying.

What do you need to believe to feel that way?

In order to be afraid of flying, or to have anxiety about it, there have to be subconscious beliefs that underpin that issue. As I've said before, most, if not all, of those beliefs are not logical. Just because those subconscious beliefs aren't logical, however, doesn't stop you from having them or being influenced by them.

When I'm working on beliefs, I often start by asking clients this simple question: "What is it that you need to believe in order to feel that way?" When I word it that way, it will often uncover things they haven't thought of before.

Imagine you're worried about a job interview, and you ask yourself "What is it that I need to believe, in order to be worried about my job interview?" You might reply "I need to believe that I'm not good enough. I need to believe I'm going to get judged. I need to believe that failure is not okay."

> What do you need to believe in order to be afraid of flying? *E.g. "I need to believe that I'm not safe," or "I need to believe that I won't be able to cope if I panic," and so on.*
> Write down the answer.
> We need to make sure you uncover all your beliefs around this, so what else do you need to believe in order to be afraid of flying?
> Repeat that question until you can't think of anything new.

You can also use questions to dig deeper into the answers. For example, one of the answers might be "I need to believe I'm not safe." So, the next question would be "What do you need to believe in order to not feel safe?" and so on.

Using these questions to keep probing in this way can quickly get to the root of the issue.

Action Step 4: Uncover the Strategy of your Phobia [83]

Just because you believe something, that doesn't make it true

In the very first chapter of this book, I shared 10 common myths about flying. Of course, these aren't just myths: they're beliefs that people have about flying. But, as we saw in that chapter, they're not true.

So, think about the beliefs you have about flying as you answer the following question.

> Are you confusing feelings with facts when you think about your phobia?

Changing Beliefs 1: Challenge Everything

On my YouTube channel, I often get comments like, "I don't care what you say. You wouldn't get me on a plane because you can get hurt doing it."

There are a lot of activities where you can get hurt. So, are you also going to stop crossing the street? Driving a car? Cooking on a hob? Using knives and forks? And what about food? After all, you might get food poisoning, so you'd better stop eating.

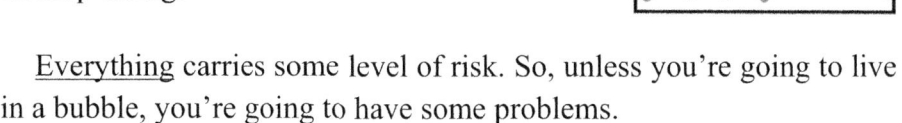

Everything carries some level of risk. So, unless you're going to live in a bubble, you're going to have some problems.

What the people leaving those comments have done is to take the belief that something—in this case flying—is dangerous, generalise it, and classify it as a fact (which it isn't). Then, because of an unconscious process that psychologists call "confirmation bias", they dismiss any positive information that contradicts that view as "untrue" and give too much attention and credibility to anything that confirms it.

Often, however, you'll find that when you challenge your own limiting beliefs, you'll come up with more resources and options. So, the next time you find yourself thinking "this is dangerous, this is scary, this should be avoided," challenge the idea: ask yourself, "Is this true? Where does that belief come from? Are there any counterexamples where it hasn't been true?"

Reframing your beliefs

Are you a glass half full or a glass half empty kind of person? Come to think of it, how can two people look at exactly the same thing and "see" something completely different? It's down to something that Milton Erickson (whom you read about in Chapter 1) called "framing".

Framing is what allows media companies to put a negative "spin" on a story to make us feel bad or a positive spin on the same story to make us feel good.

Or, as a meme I saw some time ago on Facebook put it: "If something I said can be taken two ways, and one way offends you, I probably meant the other way."

Because the truth is, whether something is good or bad, happy or sad, annoying or pleasing, is all down to the meaning *you* give it. And you choose the meaning you give to everything that happens.

Erickson told the story of two parents who came to see him about their daughter. "We're at the end of our tether," they said. "She's so wilful. She just won't do what she's told." To which Erickson replied, with a twinkle in his eye, "Well, aren't you wonderful parents, raising your daughter to be so strong and independent."

But what does any of this have to do with flying?

Imagine you're in the airport and you spot armed police, sniffer dogs, metal detectors, and all the other security paraphernalia. Instead of thinking "Oh gosh, there must be something wrong, look at all this security," you could say to yourself, Great, it's really safe here."

When your flight is delayed, you could choose to think, "I'm glad they've taken extra time to make sure everything is perfect before take-off, even though it's costing them time and money."

When you look out of the window and realise how high you're flying, you could choose to think, "Look at me, I'm soaring like an eagle!"

Instead of thinking of yourself as trapped in a steel tube, reframe it as "I'm wrapped in a cocoon of safety."

When turbulence hits and the plane starts to jostle, think, "Whee! This is like surfing!"

In the space below, or on a separate sheet of paper, write down some of your negative beliefs and thoughts about flying.

When you've finished the list, take your pen, cross each belief or thought out, and write below it an alternative, positive meaning.

Reframing is a good start to changing your beliefs. However, it's not always enough, which is why we often need therapeutic intervention processes to fully change those beliefs. In the next section, you'll get to work on yourself with one of those processes.

Changing Beliefs 2: Tapping Yourself Free

There are a number of therapies that are based on the idea of "tapping", including Emotional Freedom Technique (EFT), Thought Field Therapy (TFT), and meridian tapping. The power of these techniques is that when you use a self-soothing mechanism such as tapping while thinking about a belief or fear, it removes the emotional "charge" that you've attached to it.

Go back to the list of beliefs you wrote earlier above – the original beliefs before you reframed them.

> As you say that Belief in your head, what emotion comes up?
>
> Rate that emotion out of 10 (0= no emotion 10 = the most)
>
> **Hand**: Take 2 fingers of one hand and tap on the side of the other hand on the part you would use if you were going to chop wood karate-style.
>
> Say the belief out loud, and keep repeating it as you do the following.
>
> **Fingers**: Tap each finger on either side of the nail.

Eyebrow: Tap just above and to one side of your nose, at the beginning of the eyebrow.

Side of the Eye: Tap on the bone bordering the outside corner of each eye.

Under the Eye: Tap on the bone under each eye about 1" below the pupil.

Under the Nose: Tap on the indentation between the bottom of your nose and the top of your upper lip.

Chin: Tap midway between the point of your chin and the bottom of your lower lip.

Collar Bone: Tap on the junction where the sternum (breastbone), collarbone and the first rib meet.

Under the Arm: Tap on the side of the body, about 4 inches below the armpit.

Top of the Head: Hold your fingers together back-to-back and tap all over the top of your head.

Finally, **say that belief out loud again**. Out of 10, how strong is the emotion now?

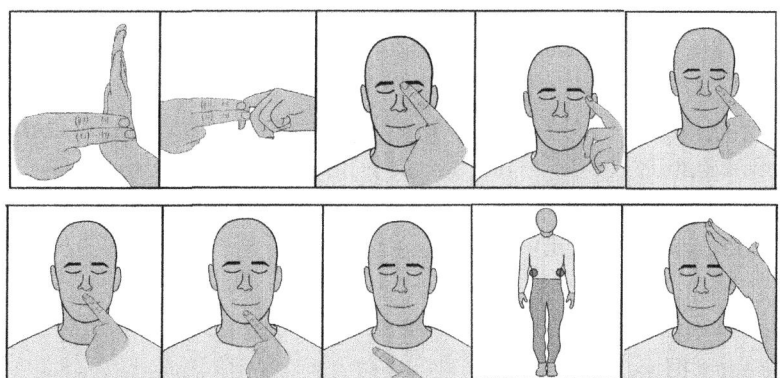

> *Now, what normally happens is that as you go through the exercise, the emotional impact of the belief gets less, and less, and less. Sometimes, the emotion lessens, and something else comes up. If your mind has wandered to an emotional event, whether you know why or not, it's probably significant.*

Repeat the process until the belief feels unimportant.

Once this happens, start again with the next belief on your list.

If the emotion doesn't change, it may be that you have a strong secondary gain from this belief, in which case take a look at Action Step 3 again.

After the last tap, take a deep breath in and shake off any feelings that remain.

Images

Here's the funny thing about movies. Most people grew up watching them, and we know that when Superman flies, it's all done with wires or computer effects. When the hero gets shot at by 20 bad guys and miraculously survives, but then he picks them off one by one with a single shot, we know it's just a bit of fantasy.

So why, when they see a plane going down in a movie, do some people immediately think, "That's real. It happens all the time."

It's not real. It's a storyline. A script.

And the great thing about scripts is they can be rewritten if the audience doesn't like them.

What's the movie in your head?

In my live events, I'll often ask the audience what pictures they see in their mind when they think about flying, and what sounds they hear. Typically, they'll say things like "the plane falling into the sea", "the plane rocking", "everyone on the plane panicking", "all the oxygen masks falling down onto the passengers", "people screaming". With things like that going around in their head, is it any surprise they're afraid of flying?

A big part of the reason you feel fear is that, at the moment when you think about flying, your mind creates a horror movie. In other words, your mind starts to create sounds and pictures that end up leaving you afraid and thinking "What am I going to do?"

That can all change, however. If you switch those sounds and pictures and even the sequence that you notice them, you can create a completely different meaning.

> So, when you think about flying, what pictures do YOU see in your mind? What sounds do you hear?

Changing your inner experience

The images and sounds we create have certain qualities. For example, the images can be bright or dim, still like a photograph or moving like a movie, in colour or black and white. Sounds can be loud or soft, clear or dull, inside your head or coming from a particular direction, they may sound like someone or something specific, and so on.

We call these qualities "submodalities". And (going back to our recipe analogy), just as the taste and texture of our cake might change if we use brown sugar instead of white, or hot milk instead of cold, how we feel about a situation can change if we alter the submodalities of the mental imagery we are creating.

> As you think about your fear of flying, notice where the fearful image is: is it close up or far away? Is the image bright or dull?
>
> Now let's change that image.
>
> If the image is in colour, change it to black and white. If it is moving, stop it.
>
> What would happen if you made it small: if you made it into a tiny, tiny dot?
>
> Now throw it off into the distance, so it ends up way off, behind a wall.
>
> Now take that tiny dot and tower over it like a giant looking down on it.
>
> What would happen if you took that image and threw it off into the sun, how would you feel differently now?
>
> What other changes could you make?
>
> Finish the exercise by shaking off any remaining emotions.
>
> What did you notice as you made changes? What happened to your level of fear of flying? Which changes made the fear diminish and were there any that made it increase?

Thoughts and Self-talk

Next, we are going to deal with your internal voice: the voice you hear in your head when you speak to yourself. Often when you're scared, fearful or anxious, you have a voice in your head saying things like, "This spider might be poisonous," "This dog is going to eat me," "Everyone in this audience is laughing at me," or, of course, "Oh no, this plane's going to crash!"

That voice can have a lot of power over you, especially if you're repeating things over and over again inside your head. But we can take that power away if we change how the voice sounds.

So, let's do that now.

> Place your feet firmly on the ground, close your eyes, and just become aware of your internal voice.
>
> Think about your fear of flying. Notice what you say to yourself in order to be afraid. Perhaps it is something like "I'm not safe, we might crash." Become aware of that internal dialogue, that self-talk, and ask yourself "Whose voice is that?"
>
> Notice the qualities of the voice: whose voice it is; the tonality; the volume (is it loud or quiet?); where it is located (Which ear is it in? Is it behind you or in front of you? Is it in your head or somewhere else?).
>
> First, let's play with the location of the voice.
>
> Imagine moving it from one side to the other or moving it behind you
>
> Push it off far away from you until it becomes a tiny, distant echo.
>
> How would that change how you feel?
>
> How would it be if the voice in your head had no gravitas, no power? How much control would that voice have over you?
>
> Let's change the voice and see.
>
> First, make it sound like the most boring person you've ever heard—perhaps a really dull teacher you remember from school. For example, if you're saying, "We're going to crash," how would that sound in that most boring voice?
>
> Now, make the voice whiny.

> Then make it high pitched and squeaky, as if a chipmunk or Mickey Mouse was giving you the narration.
>
> What happens when you play with the voice that way? How does it feel different?
>
> Shake off any emotions.

As you altered the quality of the sound, notice how much less power it had. You may have found that the feelings became weaker or even insignificant. Indeed, it can almost be laughable so you can't take that voice seriously the next time you get scared.

Posture

As we saw in chapter four, what you do with your body has a major influence on your state. By the same token, of course, your state also influences your body. Whenever you think of something that you are scared, fearful or phobic of, it gets reflected in your physiology. You will move in a certain way and adopt a particular posture: head down, and shoulders slumped.

So, when you're nervous on a flight, you probably sit forward in the seat gripping the armrest as though it has some magical power to keep the plane in the air.

If you are in a hyperalert state, your amygdala prepares to trigger the fight, flight or freeze response. By changing your body language, you can turn off the preparation signals and disarm your amygdala.

So, if when you feel that fear, you instead open up your body language – uncross your legs, sit back as though you're on the beach about to sunbathe, and open your hands as though you're about to do yoga – your mind will follow suit and relax, just as we saw in Chapter Four.

Breathing

Another simple change you can make to your physiology to reduce feelings of fear or anxiety—and one of the most underutilised—is to change your breathing.

Think about it. How do you breathe when you're stressed? If you're like most people, then either you don't breathe at all, or you breathe very rapidly and shallowly. Now, contrast that with how you breathe when you're relaxed, which for most people is slowly and deeply, with your diaphragm.

Diaphragmatic Breathing

Diaphragmatic breathing – breathing with your belly – is another ancient technique that has been practised in many cultures. In Hawaiian Huna, it is known as "Ha breathing". In ancient China, where it was called "the Lion breath", legend has it that it was a closely guarded secret of the Imperial household: anyone who taught it to an outsider would be put to death instantly.

So, I'm about to risk my life to help you overcome your fear of flying! Let's hope there are no ninjas waiting for me after I finish writing this chapter!

Just as replacing a fearful physiology with a positive or relaxed physiology can reduce fear, so replacing fearful (rapid, shallow) breathing with relaxed breathing will change your state and turn off the fight, flight or freeze response. When you feel your fear kick in, and your breathing becomes shallow, one of the easiest and most effective ways to deal with it is simply to take deep diaphragmatic breaths. Breathe in through your nose for five seconds, hold it for five seconds, and then exhale through your mouth for five seconds.

> **Step 1** – Take a deep breath in as you slowly count to five and just push your stomach out as you inhale. It can be helpful if you imagine there's a balloon in your stomach, and that as you breathe in, the balloon is getting inflated through your navel.
>
> **Step 2** – Hold the breath for five seconds (or as long as is comfortable—if you start to turn blue, it's time to breathe out!)
>
> **Step 3** – Then breathe out slowly for a count of five seconds. And if you allow your shoulders to relax as you do it, you should find you can get more connected.
>
> Keep repeating the process, breathing in slowly on a count of five allowing oxygen to fill your belly, holding for a count of five, and exhaling for a count of five. With each repetition, you'll notice yourself becoming more relaxed.

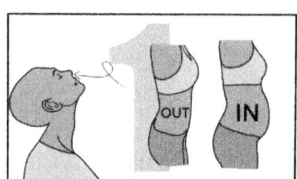 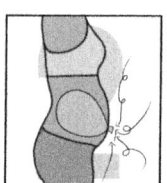 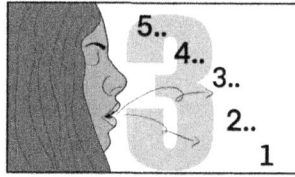

Triggers

Next, it's time to think about what triggers your anxiety, fear or phobia—not the big picture "flying", but the details of specific situations. Just like the bell that made Pavlov's dogs salivate, all kinds of things can trigger the fear response in your mind. For you, it might be a particular smell (for example, the in-flight meal being heated), or a sound (such as the 'ding' of the seatbelt sign). Or it might be something else.

While stimulus-response is often set up accidentally or subconsciously, as we saw earlier in the book, we can also artificially create our own stimulus-response to positive feelings such as excitement, enthusiasm, happiness.

To do this, we take intentional steps to get ourselves into that positive state, and we anchor it. The idea behind anchoring is that if you do something very exciting, relaxing or joyous, and you perform a unique action at the moment when that feeling is at its peak, then in future whenever you perform that action again, you'll be back in that peak state. What kind of actions? It could be something like pulling your earlobe or touching your finger and forefinger together, or making a fist with your hand.

So, let's create our own stimulus-response to feel good.

> Start by recalling a time when you felt calm, centred, and at peace (if you cannot think of a specific time, imagine what it would be like to feel this way).
>
> Notice what was going on around you: what you were seeing, what you were hearing, what you were saying to yourself, and any smells or tastes that went with it. Notice how you were breathing and how you were sitting or standing.
>
> Allow yourself to fully re-experience those feelings of calm and peace, and when the feelings are at their peak, squeeze your fist tightly, hold it, and release it just as the feelings start to fade.
>
> Stand up and shake off the feeling.
>
> Next, recall another time when you couldn't stop laughing—perhaps you'd seen your favourite comedian telling a hilarious joke,

or maybe something had just happened. Once again, notice what was going on around you: what you were seeing, what you were hearing, what you were saying to yourself, and any smells or tastes that went with it. Notice how you were breathing and how you were sitting or standing.

If you find yourself laughing now, go with it. Allow yourself to laugh just as you did back then. And, once again, as the feeling approaches its peak, squeeze your hand tightly into a fist, hold it, and release it as the emotion starts to fade.

Stand up and shake off the feeling.

Now, remember a time when you felt genuinely cared for and nurtured. Go back to that time and notice how you felt, what you were seeing, what you were hearing, what you were saying to yourself, and any smells or tastes that went with it. Notice how you were breathing and how you were sitting or standing.

Once again, as the feeling approaches its peak, squeeze your hand tightly into a fist, hold it, and release it as the emotion starts to fade.

Stand up and shake off the feeling.

Finally, remember a time when you felt totally connected to someone or something: it could be a loved one, a friend, a pet, or something else. What matters is the feeling of total connection. Go back to that time and notice how you felt, what you were seeing, what you were hearing, what you were saying to yourself, and any smells or tastes that went with it. Notice how you were breathing and how you were sitting or standing.

Once again, as the feeling approaches its peak, squeeze your hand tightly into a fist, hold it, and release it as the emotion starts to fade.

Stand up and shake off the feeling.

You've just set up an anchor with four positive states—and by the way, you can use any states you want, and you can add more states to the same anchor. But for now, let's test it.

> Without thinking of anything in particular, squeeze your fist together just like you did before. This time, you may notice that you start to feel calm, loved, and connected. And you may also notice that you feel like laughing. That's your anchor being triggered.

Feelings

All of these processes are ultimately designed to change how we feel about flying, and therefore how our mind and body react to it.

Emotions like fear create physical sensations within your body – butterflies, chills, heat, or whatever – that literally tell you that you're "feeling" fear. So, let's start by identifying what your fear of flying feels like to you.

> Ask yourself:
> *What do I feel when I'm fearful?*
> *Where do I feel it?*
> *How intense is it?*

Changing Your Feelings: Part 1

In a moment, you're going to allow your eyes to scan slowly and find where in that scan a particular memory feels strongest. Once you've identified that point, I'll show you how easy it is to reduce the negative feelings that accompany that memory.

Think about your fear of flying.

1. Slowly move your eyes left to right as though you were following an imaginary line or horizon and notice how intense the memory is at each point along the line. Stop wherever the negative feeling is the strongest.

2. Now imagine a vertical line crossing that imaginary horizon at the point where the feelings were strongest. Still thinking about your fear of flying, and without moving your eyes left or right, slowly scan up and down that vertical line and notice that as you do so, the feelings will change in intensity. Stop wherever the feeling is strongest.

3. Finally, imagine a line going straight from your eyes to that point where the feelings were strongest. Without changing the direction in which your eyes are looking, focus your gaze at a point on that line very close to you. As you continue thinking about your fear of flying, gradually shift your focus further out along the line, and again notice where the feelings are strongest.

You've now pinpointed where in 3-dimensional space your feelings about your fear of flying are most intense.

Now ask yourself, how strong are the negative feelings on a scale from 0 to 10?

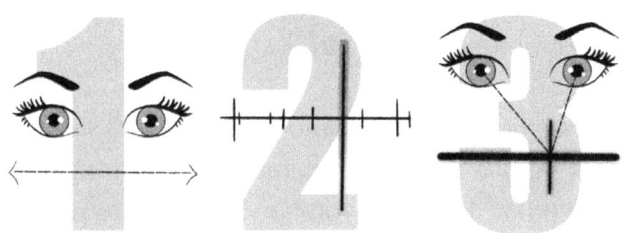

4. Hold your attention on that spot and focus on the feelings and images that represent your fear of flying. After a short time, you'll notice that the feelings should start to lessen. Do this for a few mins then check in again. Where is the feeling now on a scale from 0 to 10?

5. Next, keeping your head pointing straight ahead, move your eyes in a smooth arc from fully left, across the bridge of your nose, to fully right, then back. Repeat that for a few minutes.

6. Then, keeping your head level, look up as though you were trying to see the inside of your eyelids, and rotate your eyes in a full circle, first clockwise then anti-clockwise, ten times in each direction.

7. Finally, again keeping your head straight and level, look up, then sweep your eye in an arc down all the way, then back up to the top. Repeat this ten times.

Scan your body. How strong is the feeling now on a scale from 0 to 10? You can repeat this process as many times as you need to.

Changing Your Feelings: Part 2

1. Focus on the feeling that comes up when you think about your fear of flying. Become aware of how the feeling moves around your body. Does it move clockwise or anticlockwise?

2. Now focus on the feeling. Take the feeling out of your body and spin it in front of you like a wheel. Follow the movement with your hand.
3. That feeling has a colour. Become aware of the colour, then change it to something more pleasing – bright white is often a good colour to change it to.
4. Now reverse the direction of the spin, and again, follow it with your hand.
5. Pull the feeling back into the body, still spinning it in the opposite direction.
6. Spin it faster and faster until it disappears.

Changing Your Feelings: Part 3

We all have times when we feel things are getting to us, so I'm about to teach you a very sophisticated tool for calming yourself.

The following actions are taken with your eyes closed, so read the description several times and make sure you understand precisely what you have to do.

Are you ready? …

Action Step 4: Uncover the Strategy of your Phobia [101]

> 1. Close your eyes and think about your fear. Whatever comes up for you, cross your arms and put one hand on each shoulder. Now move your hands all the way down your arms to your fingers, and then back up again.

In psychology, we have a very complicated name for this action. It's called a "hug". If, when you feel unsafe, you give yourself a hug, it reassures and soothes you.

Now, here's step 2 in the technique.

> 2. Slowly stroke your cheeks with the back of your hands, still holding the eyes in the same place, do this for a few mins. Where is the feeling now on a scale from 0 to 10?

 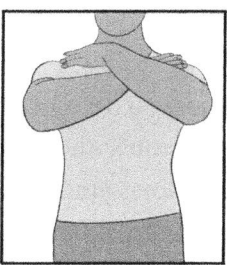 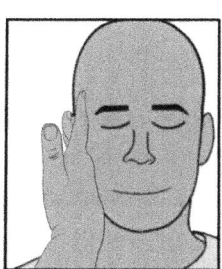

Using this self-soothing mechanism while focusing on your fear will often take out the emotional charge. It works by activating the body's mechanism for releasing hormones that decrease blood pressure and heart rate and induce a relaxation response: the parasympathetic nervous system. Strangely enough, this is also the system responsible for sexual arousal, digestion, and defecation!

Putting it All Together

If you had to teach someone the recipe for your phobia, what would you teach them? As I said earlier, there is a strategy or recipe for everything we do in our lives, from brushing our teeth to putting our socks on in the morning. And, as we've seen, there is a sequence and a strategy that you have to follow, and a set of ingredients—thoughts, feelings, how you breathe, move, and hold yourself—you have to use to be afraid.

That means, of course, that you can also learn how to not be afraid. When you meet someone who doesn't have a fear of flying, don't just say to them, "Oh, you're so lucky." Instead, ask them what they do in their head when they think about flying: what do they think about, what do they feel, what images do they make in their head, and what beliefs do they have about flying? Your goal is to find out what's going on internally for them in order for them to enjoy flying: find out their recipe and learn it.

Keeping a phobia going, as you've seen, takes a lot of work and skill. Even at my age, I barely remember the plot of the last film I watched. And yet, when you have a phobia, you can create vivid movies in your head full of sounds, images, and feelings, and rerun them perfectly over and over again. You remember exactly what you need to do to be afraid every time. That ability to never forget is a fantastic skill, and it's one that you could just as easily apply to something else in your life that could help you.

CHAPTER EIGHT

Action Step 5: Transforming the Past

So far, we've been working on the movie that you run in your head when you're scared. But, of course, to create these images, thoughts, feelings, and beliefs about flying, there usually has to be something in your past that triggers this behaviour. And, as we saw earlier in this book, there can be a direct or indirect link from the event to your phobia.

In this chapter, we're going to go back and work on your memories of the event that first created your phobia: the time when you first learned to be afraid of flying.

We've already seen that very often when we are fearful, we make big bright pictures in our mind that end up making us even more frightened. We've also seen that if we change the images associated with the fear – make them black and white, move them about, make them funny, etc. – we change the underlying feelings and take out the negative emotional charge.

Scrambling Past Memories

Research shows that when we see something for the first time, our visual cortex initially becomes highly activated. Usually, this reaction fades over time. With fearful memories, however, the visual cortex is activated just as strongly every time you think of them, as though you were seeing the event for the first time. Fortunately for us, that also means that processes which scramble visual memory can be very effective in transforming your phobias.

1. Imagine you are sitting in a cinema looking at a blank screen. Make the cinema look just perfect for you, and imagine that the seat is the comfiest you have ever sat in.
2. When you're happy with the theatre and your seat, imagine floating up out of your body and into the projection booth, high above all the seats in the cinema so that you can look back and see yourself sitting in the cinema looking at the screen.
3. When was the very first time you created your fear of flying? What was the very first event? In your own time, let your mind wander back—and if you cannot remember that very first time, focus on a significant event that you do remember.

Notice the feelings that come up as you think about that event. On a scale of 0 to 10 (0 being not at all, 10 being the highest), how strong is the feeling?

4. In a moment, a black and white movie is going to play on the screen. When that happens, I don't want you to watch the screen. Instead, you're going to look back down from the projection booth to where you are sitting in the theatre and just watch yourself sitting there calmly in the cinema, watching the screen that is playing the movie.
5. The movie that is going to play on the screen is of the time when you first felt a fear of flying, from the moment just before the event happened through to the moment afterwards when you were safe.
6. So, when you're ready, watch yourself as the movie starts to play in black and white. Remember: look back down from the projection booth to where you are sitting in the theatre and just watch yourself sitting there calmly in the cinema, watching the screen that is playing the movie.

7. When the movie comes to an end, and you're safe again, white-out the screen.
8. Float back down into your seat from the projection booth and then float out of your seat and into the screen so that you put yourself inside the movie.
9. Once you're there, run the film at high speed backwards in colour from the end—the time when you were safe after the event—back to the beginning, before it all happened.
10. When you get back to the beginning of the movie, white-out the screen once more.
11. Float back out of the screen, down into your seat, and then back up into the projection booth.
12. Again, look down from the elevated projection booth to where you are seated calmly watching the phobic event play out on the screen as you run the movie forwards in black and white to the end. When it's finished, white-out the screen.

Repeat steps 9 to 12, making sure to speed up the backwards movie in Step 9. Make it run backwards at 5-times normal speed and, as you do, add comedy music and images. Could you add some furry animal ears? Could you add a fast, squeaky voice? Could you add other people or things to the situation to make it even more comical? Could you change the speed so that everyone is moving comically fast, like an old silent movie?

When the emotion of the phobia has lessened, imagine floating up above the whole thing and ask yourself, 'What learning can I take from this event that will help me in future?'

Some people are able to do this process just once and get instant results. For others, it takes a little getting used to – there's a lot to do setting up the cinema screen and playing through the scenario – so practice the steps until you get the hang of the technique.

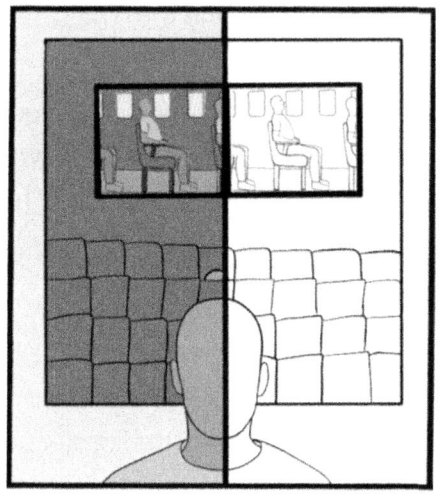

Do the Time Warp

Our next technique is very sci-fi: we're going to change time itself. We can do this because humans store emotions in lines that we call timelines. We're not consciously aware of those lines, but we can bring them into our awareness with a simple exercise. It's a closed-eye process, so, again, you'll need to read through the instructions several times and memorise the steps

> 1. Close your eyes and think back to your 21st birthday.
> 2. As you think about that memory, you'll notice that it's located somewhere in space. You might be aware of the memory being in front of you, behind you or to one side, or it may even be inside you. Also, notice where it is vertically: is it above you, below you, or on the same level?

Action Step 5: Transforming the Past [107]

3. Once you've located that memory of your 21st birthday, think about your 16th birthday, and notice where it is located.
4. And if you didn't notice it before, notice now the relationship between the two memories and where they are stored.
5. Next, whatever age you are now, think about that birthday, and notice how that is stored in your mind.
6. If you focus on those three memories, could they describe a line? It might be a straight line, or it might be a curve, but if you put them in order—your 16th birthday, your 21st birthday, and your last birthday, you'll notice they are on a line.
7. And if you know where the line is for your past, you can also work out where the line is that stretches out into your future. So, do that now. Imagine an event you know is coming up in the next week – maybe a meeting, or a meal with friends. Notice where it is. Then imagine an event a month from now, and then one a year from now. Each time, do the same as you did for the past and notice the line for your future.

Once you've identified where your timeline is, you can open your eyes and come back to full awareness.

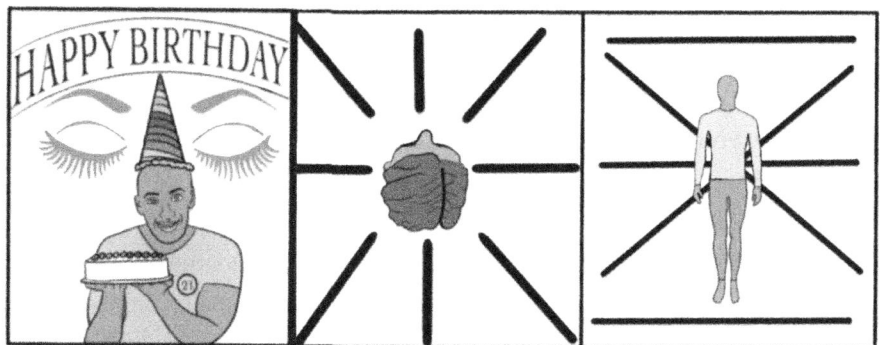

> **Let me guide you**
>
> Many of the techniques in this book were designed for you to listen to the instructions and follow along. To make things easier for you, I've created recordings of all the processes. To find out how to get your own copy, visit www.FaceYourFearOfFlying.com/virtual

The Temporal Reprocessing Method

> Chris told me to imagine myself watching certain incidents that frightened me from a bird's eye perspective. Imagining it in this way, you can re-examine frightening events in your past (like my difficult flight), but without the stress. For me, I could see that my flight was perfectly safe, the turbulence was totally normal, and that nothing bad was going to happen to me.
> **Emmy Griffiths, Hello Magazine**

As we saw earlier in the book, your fear was created by a significant event in your past—you can think of it as the trigger or seed for your phobia. There may be multiple significant events in your past related to your fear, but there will be one, way back, that started it all. And, because of the way your mind stores memories, if we can clear that event from your timeline, it will cause the others to fall away.

To clear the event, we are going to float above our timeline and travel back to that very first event as observers so that we can take positive lessons, learnings, and insights from it. Then we will come back along the timeline to the present, learning from and clearing all the similar events that have happened since then. And because our mind is the only thing capable of travelling faster than the speed of light, we can do all of that in minutes rather than decades.

Finding the first event

For this exercise, we're going to use the subconscious yes/no signal you discovered back in Action Step 3 (Chapter Six).

1. Ask yourself "do I know the very first event – not the most significant, but the very first event – that led to my fear of flying?
2. Wait for a yes signal – you will get this eventually, as all memories are in your mind somewhere, although you probably aren't aware of them.
3. Now ask yourself how old you were. Ask for a "yes" for each year of the age you were (i.e. if you were four years old, you'll get "yes" four times).

Another way to locate that first event is to move forward from birth, year by year, which is the next technique.

1. Ask "Was I newly born when I first created my fear of flying?" and wait for a yes/no signal.
2. If the answer is "no", move on: "Was I one year old?" and again wait for a yes/no signal.

3. If the answer is still "no", ask "Was I two years old?" and wait for a yes/no signal.
4. Keeping increasing the age, year by year, until you get a "yes".

> *Note: You may get a "yes" signal but not know or see what the root event is. If that happens, you may find it will become clear in the next process, but it's not necessary to know the exact event in order to remove the emotional charge from the past.*

Removing the Charge from the Root Event

Now that we've identified how old you were when your fear of flying first arose, and perhaps even pinpointed a specific event that caused it, we can take away it's power by removing the emotional charge associated with the past.

> **Step 1** – Imagine your life is a line on the floor, following the shape you discovered above. Stand at the point on this line that represents "now" and walk backwards along the line until you reach the age you identified in the previous process (you may feel a pull in your body when you feel you're in the right place).
>
> **Step 2** – Stepping off the line, move away as far as you need to in order to not to feel any negative emotions about the event and watch from a distance.
>
> **Step 3** – Ask yourself "On a scale of 1 to 10, how strong are the emotions in this event?"
>
> **Step 4** – As you watch your younger self, what can the older you teach the younger you to help let go of that fear of flying?
>
> **Step 5** – If you could have brought a mentor or guide to that event, what advice would they give you to help you look at the situation differently?

Step 6 – Take five deep breaths, step back into the event, dart your eyes left and right ten times, then step out of the event and watch the event from a distance again.

Step 7 – Imagine a colour of relaxation and beam it into the event so it fills the whole event and floods it with light.

Step 8 – Imagine stepping back from the event further back in time and watching it before it ever happened. On a scale from 0 to 10, how strong are the emotions now? If the emotions are at 0, move to step 9. If not, repeat steps 2 to 8 again.

If you find you are still having trouble getting to 0, it may be that this is not the first event. Try walking back further.

Step 9 – Once the emotions are at 0, start slowly walking forward from this first event to the present, noticing all the other events through your life where you had these similar emotions.

Step 10 – When you find one of these later events, repeat steps 2-8 for each event until you get back to now.

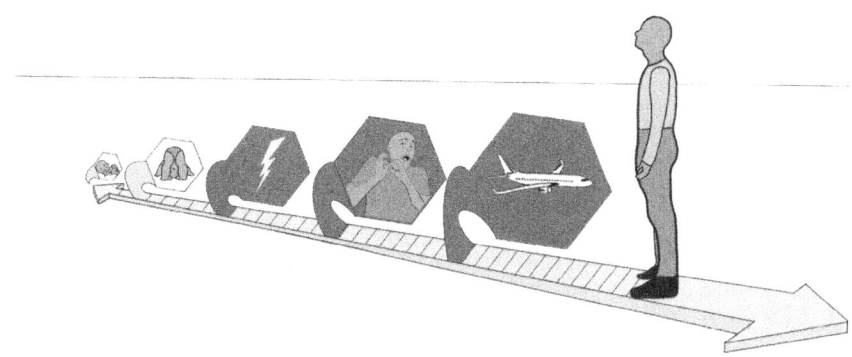

Done right, this process should feel like a "defrag" for your mind and can leave you feeling either extremely energised or relaxed.

CHAPTER NINE

Action Step 6: Change your Stimulus-Response

We've already seen the importance of the movies and imagery that you are putting into your mind. To see how powerful these can be, think for a moment about professional athletes. I haven't met many runners who like to get up at 5am on a cold morning to go and train. So, imagine if, when the alarm went off, they just lay in the dark thinking about what it was going to be like running in the cold and the wet, and seeing themselves shivering and miserable. The chances are they would turn off the alarm; roll over in their nice, warm bed; and go back to sleep. And they wouldn't win many races.

So, what do professional athletes think about instead? They focus on winning. They see themselves on the podium with the gold medal around their neck. They hear the cheers of the crowd. That makes it a lot easier to get out of bed and train.

When it comes to flying, then, what are you thinking about? What would happen if, rather than seeing yourself gripping the seat, you instead focused on the reason you were flying, for example, the thought of sitting on the beach, sipping champagne, enjoying the view, and relaxing? That difference in focus will really change how you feel.

Switching the Imagery

Don't get me wrong. This isn't about turning you into one of those positive-thinking junkies, muttering "Happy thoughts. Happy thoughts. I have no problems!" to yourself, because that isn't useful either. It's about recognising that whatever you put into your mind is going to affect your state, particularly when it comes to thinking about the future. So, ask yourself: "What am I actually focussing on when I think about booking a flight? What am I putting in my mind to make myself feel bad?" And, if you were to change that, how would you feel?

With that in mind, when you think about flying, what mental images would you like to see in your mind instead? What would you like to imagine? Perhaps you might like to imagine yourself sitting on the beach relaxing, enjoying the sunshine; or maybe there's something else that would encourage you and calm you.

In this exercise, you're going to switch the imagery in your head, from the negative, fear-inducing pictures you're giving yourself, to something more positive and enticing.

Let me guide you

This is another exercise that's much easier if you follow along as I talk you through the instructions. To find out how to get your own copy, visit

www.FaceYourFearOfFlying.com/virtual

Step 1 – Make a list on a sheet of paper of the things you'd like to see when you think about flying.

Close your eyes and create a positive image of how you would like to be. Notice how you feel when you think about that. And when you've enjoyed those feelings for a little time, you can open your eyes.

Now, we're going to switch the images you've been using in the past and replace them with these positive images.

Step 2 – Think for a moment about getting on a plane right now. What do you see in your mind that makes you afraid or anxious? When you've got that in your mind's eye, take a snapshot.

Step 3 – Put this image in front of you and make it slightly see-through, as though it's being projected onto glass.

Step 4 – Leaving that image on the glass in front of you, create a small black and white "thumbnail" of the positive imagery you described in the last exercise, with all the sounds, feelings, and emotions that go with it.

Step 5 – Put the positive thumbnail down and to one side, some distance behind the glass screen.

Step 6 – Imagine a powerful spring connecting you to the thumbnail and pulling tight against it.

Step 7 – When you're ready, release the thumbnail so that the spring pulls it rapidly towards you, shattering the screen as it goes through.

Step 8 – As the new empowering image gets closer, imagine it getting bigger and brighter, and going from black and white to full colour.

Step 9 – Notice how you feel, what you see, and what you say to yourself, and lock that in your mind. Allow yourself to sit with it, see it, hear it and feel it, and when you've enjoyed it for some time, open your eyes and shake it off.

Each time you repeat the exercise, you may notice the old image is harder to bring up, or dimmer or less sharp. Keep repeating it until you find it hard to find the old negative images and feelings. When all that's left is the new, positive imagery, notice what you feel and see.

Anchoring a positive holiday

It's all very well making yourself feel good for a moment, but how do you make sure those good feelings stay so you can access them whenever you want? In this process, which is similar to the one we used in Action Step 4, you'll create a positive anchor associated with great experiences you've enjoyed, and I'll show you how you can access that anchor any time you need.

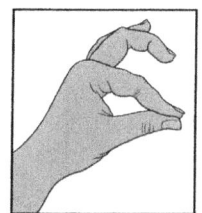

Step 1 – Pick three positive memories from past trips or holidays. If you cannot think of any, just imagine what it would be like to go on a trip you loved.

Step 2 – Starting with the earliest memory, notice what was going on around you: what you were seeing, hearing, and saying to yourself, and any smells or tastes that went with it. Notice how you were breathing and how you were sitting or standing.

Step 3 – Allow yourself to fully re-experience the positive feelings of that holiday. When the feelings are at their peak, squeeze the thumb and index finger of either hand together – many people choose the hand they write with. Press that thumb and finger together tightly, and release them just as the feelings start to fade.

Step 4 – Stand up and shake off the feelings.

Step 5 – Recall a second time you had a great holiday. Again, notice what was going on around you, how you were feeling, breathing, and how you were sitting or standing.

Step 6 – Squeeze the same thumb and finger together again tightly, hold it, and release it as the emotions start to fade.

Step 7 – Stand up and shake off the feelings.

Step 8 – Now remember a third great holiday memory and repeat step 5 to re-experience it.

Step 9 – Once again, as the feelings approach their peak, squeeze your thumb and forefinger, hold it, and release it as the emotions starts to fade.

Step 10 – Stand up and shake off the feeling.

Step 11 – Remember a time when you felt really excited about completing a task. Go back to that time and notice how you felt, what you were seeing, what you were hearing, what you were saying to yourself, and any smells or tastes that went with it. Notice how you were breathing and how you were sitting or standing.

Step 12 – Once again, as the feeling approaches its peak, squeeze your fingers tightly together, hold it, and release as the emotions start to fade.

Step 13 – Stand up and shake off the feeling.

Congratulations! You've just created a positive anchor. To test it, squeeze your finger and thumb together as you think about taking a flight. Notice how you feel differently.

CHAPTER TEN

Action Step 7: Designing Your Fear-Free Future

As we have seen, fear is not something you catch like a cold. It's something you do to yourself—albeit subconsciously—with your thoughts, your beliefs, your feelings, and your emotions.

For instance, let's say you feel great right now, but then you think "What if I don't feel like this in a week?" In order for you to feel good right now and then not feel good in a week's time, you would have to change something: the pictures you make inside your mind, your thoughts, your feelings, and your internal dialogue. In other words, you'd have to follow your emotional recipe, as we discussed in Action Step 4.

Of course, once you become aware of your negative patterns, you can start targeting and changing them. So, if you notice yourself making a negative mental movie, you can immediately begin to change it as we've seen in the book: running it backwards, messing with the soundtrack, making it black and white, pushing it out into the distance, etc.

Does thinking about your phobia help?

When I dig deeper on clients' issues to get to the subconscious roots of what is going on, I often find that they have been harbouring a belief that, if they mentally rehearse the danger, it will somehow prepare them to face it if it arises. There's a big problem with that approach: while you're running through that worst-case scenario, your brain doesn't know the difference between what is imagined and what is real. So, every time you imagine the worst-case scenario, you trigger your fear reflex, and your body releases adrenaline and other hormones that go with it, and you can end up feeling as bad as if it were happening for real.

That would be fine if it got you ready to face your danger. But, as we've already seen, that is far from the case. All those negative thoughts, images, self-talk, and everything else simply reinforce the problem.

Now, it's hard to deal with a danger when you're crippled by fear. So, the next time you find yourself thinking, "I need to be ready for this," imagine yourself completely relaxed, calm, centred, and ready. What would that do to your stress levels? How much better would you feel?

Creating a Positive Belief in the Future

We said earlier that if you try to resist your fear, it will just push back harder. Since you can't deal with the phobia of flying by resisting, what can you do instead? You have to create new positive beliefs and use them to replace your self-talk.

In this section, we'll be using the tapping techniques and eye movements you learned in Chapter Two. So, if you need to refresh your memory, go back and look at that again before you move on to this exercise.

> In the last chapter, you made a list of the things you'd like to *see* the next time you fly.
>
> On the same sheet of paper, or a new one, make a new list of the positive things you'd like to *say to yourself* the next time you fly and the positive beliefs about flying that you'd like to have.
>
> **Step 1 –** Once you've finished listing all the positive thoughts, review that list, and ask yourself, on a scale from 0 to 100%, how true does this feel right now?

Step 2 – Next, focus on those positive thoughts and beliefs you wrote down, and start to say them out loud loudly and in a clear, confident voice.

Step 3 – Keep repeating the statements, always confidently and clearly. After every couple of repetitions, rate how true the list feels to you from 0 to 100%.

Step 4 – As you continue to repeat the thoughts and beliefs on the list, start to use the technique you learned in *"Changing Your Feelings: Part 1"* in Chapter Seven. Repeat the positive belief, moving your eyes left and right ten times, then up and down ten times. Then move your eyes ten times in a circle clockwise, and finally ten times in a circle anti-clockwise

Step 5 – Next use the technique you learned in the section *"Changing Beliefs 2: Tapping Yourself Free"*, also in Chapter Seven. Repeating the positive belief out loud over and over again, do the following:

Hand: Take 2 fingers of one hand and tap on the side of the other hand on the part you would use if you were going to chop wood karate-style.

Fingers: Tap each finger on either side of the nail.

Eyebrow: Tap just above and to one side of your nose, at the beginning of the eyebrow.

Side of the Eye: Tap on the bone bordering the outside corner of each eye.

Under the Eye: Tap on the bone under each eye about 1" below the pupil.

Under the Nose: Tap on the indentation between the bottom of your nose and the top of your upper lip.

> ***Chin:*** Tap midway between the point of your chin and the bottom of your lower lip.
>
> ***Collar Bone:*** Tap on the junction where the sternum (breastbone), collarbone and the first rib meet.
>
> ***Under the Arm:*** Tap on the side of the body, about 4 inches below the armpit.
>
> ***Top of the Head:*** Hold your fingers together back-to-back and tap all around the top of your skull.
>
> *Now, I don't know how quickly your level of belief went up, but if it hasn't reached "100% True" yet, you can repeat the eyes and tapping sequences a few more times.*
>
> *Sometimes you may feel some resistance, and your inner voice starts to ask things like "But what if I panic?" "What if I'm not safe?" and so on. We will deal with that in the next section*

Anxiety, Worry, and What Ifs

There's a phrase I hear all the time from my clients: "What if?" What if the plane crashes? What if I let go of this fear and I'm not safe? What if? What if? What if? People can run these *what-ifs* hundreds of times a day for every possible scenario, especially when they are suffering from extreme anxiety. If you have a phobia, it tends to come up as you get closer to a trigger event. For example, as the day of your flight approaches, you may start to wonder, "What if the plane does this?" "What if the pilot does that?" "What if I panic?" and so on. These types of thoughts are especially common when your fear of flying is linked to anxiety in the ways we saw earlier.

In this section, we are going to work on those *what-ifs* and the recurring thoughts that prompt them.

Often, we are so used to dismissing the recurring thoughts that go with *what-ifs* as "silly" or "illogical" that we fail to even acknowledge them, but we need to bring them into our conscious awareness in order to challenge them and let them go.

> Think about any of the *what-ifs* you may have about flying and take a few moments to write them all down. For example: "What if I'm not safe?"
>
> Once you've got all the *what-ifs* down on paper, we're going to go through the list one by one and challenge each one.
>
> Look at the first statement you wrote down and ask yourself, "From 0 to 10, how likely is this *really* to happen?"
>
> When you've rated it, say it out loud and notice any feelings and emotions that go with it.
>
> Repeat the phrase out loud and go through the eye movement tapping sequences from Chapter Seven. As you keep repeating it and tapping, you should find that the emotions attached to it get weaker.
>
> When you're ready, repeat the process with the second item on the list, then the third, and so on until you run out of *what-ifs*.

As you go through the exercise, not only should you find that your limiting beliefs start to dissipate but, if you keep tapping, you should also find that the truth will come up about what's really going on: what's behind this pattern of behaviour, and the reason you have been holding on to it.

The Future Feelings Process

How would it feel to imagine the pleasure of overcoming your fear, phobia, or anxiety before it ever happened? Anxiety is really nothing more than the fear of the future; it's the anticipation of something bad happening "later". So, we can deal with it by replacing that negative future vision with a vision of something good.

In Action Step 5, I showed you how to go back into the past along your timeline and clear the negative events that created your phobia. We can also travel forward along the timeline, into the future, in the same way. For example, you can take yourself to a point in time after you've successfully completed your flight and imagine what it will be like when you're sitting on the beach, sipping your favourite cold drink and soaking up the sun. Then, you drop down into that moment and notice how you feel. Now, when you can take on those feelings and that learning of how you'll feel after the successful completion of your journey, you can let go of the anticipatory anxiety.

Let's do that now.

This is a closed-eye process, so you'll either need to memorise the steps carefully or have a partner read them to you. Alternatively, of course, you can get a recording of me walking you through the exercise (and others) at www.FaceYourFearOfFlying.com/virtual.

> Stand Up and close your eyes.
>
> **Step 1** – Think back to when you discovered your timeline in Action Step 5. Remember where your future is, where your past is, and where your present is.
>
> **Step 2** – Imagine rising up high above this moment and floating forward along your timeline to an unspecified time in the future

where you've successfully completed your flight and you're feeling relaxed and happy.

Step 3 - As you relax there, turn around and look back along your timeline to the flight that got you there. Notice how you'll feel, what you'll see, what you'll say to yourself, what you'll do, knowing that you got to your destination successfully.

Step 4 - Float down into that positive event of completing your journey and really experience those feelings. Notice how you'll breathe, how you'll move, what you'll say to yourself after successfully completing it.

Step 5 - Now, take on board those feelings. Notice all the things that go with it. What you see, how you move, what you say to yourself.

Step 6 - Float up high and come all the way back to the present with those feelings and just notice how flying seems different now.

Step 7 - Finally, open your eyes and shake it off.

Editing Your Own Future

Have you ever had a bad day, a scary experience, a bad job interview, or some other negative experience and thought to yourself, "D'oh! What was I thinking? Next time I'm not going to do that!" But what happens the next time? You find yourself doing exactly the same thing.

When your brain gets used to taking a particular path in a situation, your behaviours can become "hard-wired", and eventually the response becomes automatic. Flying, and how our subconscious mind chooses to respond to it, is no different.

When that happens, the only way to change your behaviour is rehearsal: you have to imagine being in the situation and act out the behaviour and response you want instead. Let me give you an example.

> Think of an unpleasant flight from your past. Imagine you could print that memory on an old-fashioned roll of movie film so that you can replay the entire experience in your mind.
>
> Now, even with the worst experiences, it would be unusual for everything to have been terrible: some things will have gone better than others, especially at the start. So, run the film through in your mind and notice what was good and went well.
>
> At some point, of course, you'll get to something that makes you think, "I didn't handle that well. I wish I hadn't done that." For example, you might remember sitting in the seat on the plane shaking, gripping the armrest, and squeezing your eyes shut.
>
> The great thing about working with a roll of film is that you can take a razor blade and cut the film just before that bit you don't like and just after it, and you can lift out that whole section of film and replace it with how you wish the scene had gone.
>
> How would you like to act instead? What would you like to think, do, and say? How would you be moving and breathing? How loud would the sounds be? How bright would the colours be?
>
> For example, maybe you wish you'd been relaxed in your seat, breathing easily, looking out of the window at the bright blue sky and enjoying the view.
>
> Once you've got the scene exactly as you want it, just like a great editor, you're going to take that new piece of film and place it into your trip. Then you can rewind the movie and play it all the way through—and this time, notice how it feels different. It may take you a few attempts to get the film just right, and that's perfectly OK.

Play that movie backwards and forwards a few times, and once you're happy with that scene, go forwards in the movie until you find the next section where you think, "I could have done that differently."

Once again, cut out the scene you don't like, and create a new version that reflects what you wish you had said, thought, and done. When you've got it just right, edit it into the movie and play the movie through a few times.

Keep going until you reach the end of the experience and you've replaced all the sections you're not happy with, and when the whole experience is just right for you, play it forwards from the start to the end and notice how it feels.

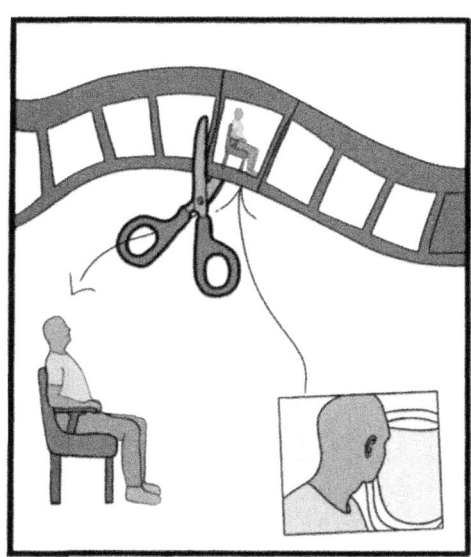

This exercise will hardwire the new behaviour into your mind so that in the future, when you find yourself in a similar situation, you can be the way you want to and start reacting differently.

CHAPTER ELEVEN

Preparing for Your Flight

Even if you've worked through the book, you may find some of your old patterns try to return when you plan to take a flight. So, in this chapter, we're going to take everything you've learned in the earlier parts of the book and apply them as the day of your flight gets close.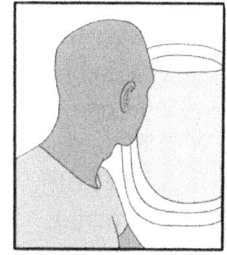

Too often, people get in touch with me just before their flight to ask for help, even though they were aware of their fear a month before and could have taken action then.

Don't leave dealing with your fear of flying to the last moment. In the time leading up to your flight, it's good to work on any fears, worries, or negative emotions that are coming up before you travel. The mistake a lot of people make is that they try and ignore those feelings, and they just keep getting stronger. The key is to work on those negative thoughts or feelings the second you notice them creeping in: "eat the frog while it's a tadpole!"

Upcoming flight process – Part 1

There are many stages in the process of taking a flight. Think about each stage in the following table and notice that some stages are less scary than others. Against each stage, rate your level of fear from 0 to 10 and write it into the table (of course, if you've followed the exercises in this book, your remaining level of fear should be quite low).

STAGE	Level of fear
Booking the ticket	/10
Travelling to the airport	/10
Checking in	/10
Going through security	/10
Waiting at the gate	/10
Boarding	/10
Watching the door close	/10
Taxying	/10
Listening to the safety talk	/10
Take off	/10
Cruising	/10
Landing	/10
Any other aspects of flying that are significant to you	
	/10
	/10
	/10

In Action Step 6 you created a positive anchor by squeezing together your thumb and forefinger. In the following exercise, you'll use that anchor to reduce any remaining fear you identified in the table above.

> Think about an upcoming flight.
>
> Run through the stages of that future flight like a movie in your mind. As you go through the movie, any time you notice negative thoughts or feelings fire off your positive anchor by squeezing your thumb and forefinger together. Keep squeezing until the negative emotion goes away. Once it does, rewind the movie and play that part again. Notice how you feel differently. If the emotion isn't at zero (or very low), repeat these steps until it is.
>
> Once the emotion is gone, start moving forward again through the movie of your future flight, and repeat the process any time where negative thoughts or emotions come up for you.

> N.B. Over time, your anchor may weaken. If you notice that squeezing your thumb and forefinger isn't reducing the intensity of your negative emotions, go back to Action Step 6 and top up your anchor.

Upcoming flight process – Part 1

Next, you'll replace the negative emotions with positive ones.

> Once you've been through the whole movie of your future flight and all the negative emotions are low, take a long, slow, deep breath in through your nose and imagine the air filling up your stomach and heart.
>
> When your stomach and heart are full, breathe out slowly through your mouth. Repeat this breathing five times, and as the air flows, think of how relaxed you'll feel after you have travelled. Bring back the positive memory from earlier, like sitting on the beach, and focus on all the things you are happy and grateful for.
>
> Now, holding on to the positive feelings, run through the whole journey one more time and notice how much better you can feel.

The day of your flight

It's still possible that unhelpful thoughts or feelings might pop up on the day of your flight. If they do, you can deal with them by applying some of the techniques you've learned in this book. Here are some helpful steps you can take in the moment. Find which work best for you and combine them as needed to create your most enjoyable flight experience.

- Remind yourself how safe flying really is (Chapter One).
- Open your awareness (Chapter Four).

- If the negative thoughts have a voice, play with the volume and make it sound comical (Chapter Seven).
- Challenge any negative beliefs (Chapter Seven).
- If any negative images come up in your mind, make them black and white. Make them tiny and push them out into the distance (Chapter Seven).
- Use the eye movement and tapping techniques (Chapter Seven).
- Change your posture and breathing (Chapter Seven).
- Spin the feeling (Chapter Seven).
- Fire your positive anchor (Chapter Nine).

After the flight

Well done! You took the flight, and whether it went well, badly, or indifferently, you should congratulate yourself. You did it!

So, what can you do to make the next one even better still (apart from practising the processes in this book, of course!)?

It's worth anchoring any positive feelings you have if you feel great just after the flight or later when you're enjoying the sites, the beach or whatever. Use the techniques in Chapter Nine to set up that anchor.

> NOTE: If the emotion is more like relief that you got through the flight, don't anchor it: you'd just be anchoring tension, and it will not work as well.

Also, if there are any stages of the flight where you would have liked to have acted differently, it's worth doing the *Editing Your Own Future* process from Chapter Ten. Often, just saying to yourself "I'll do it differently next time" is not enough. Instead, mentally rehearse what you'd do differently.

Conclusion

Congratulations on making it to this point in the book and overcoming your fear of flying.

Speaking from my own experience, since overcoming my fear of flying I've travelled the world, seen sights I could never have visited, and enjoyed vacations in places that were off-limits to me.

And I've seen thousands of clients for whom similar opportunities opened up once they had reprogrammed their flying phobia using the tools I have taught you.

If you have worked through the exercises and put in the effort, you will find that flying becomes effortless and enjoyable, and you can get back (or get for the first time) the life you want.

Often, it's only when you have that freedom that you realise just how much your old fears and worries held you back; all the things you were missing out on; all the things you wanted to do but couldn't because there was a block.

And when you can overcome that block… the sky's the limit!

To continue on this journey, if you have other fears you need to work on, or if you feel you want some more personal help, you can book a free Clarity Call with me.

Visit ChristopherPaulJones.com/free-clarity-call/ to get started.

ABOUT THE AUTHOR

Who is Chris Jones?

Christopher Paul Jones, The Breakthrough Expert, is a Speaker, Trainer, Therapist, and Developer of the Integrated Change System™. His work has been featured regularly on international TV, radio and in the press, including the BBC, Channel 4, Canada's CBC, Hello, GQ, Harpers Bazaar, Marie Claire, and national newspapers. Christopher's clients come from all over the world to see him in his consulting rooms on London's world-renowned Harley Street, and have included Hollywood actors and Oscar nominees, models, musicians, presenters, and celebrities.

Never one to follow the status quo, Christopher pioneered an integrated approach combining mainstream psychology with cutting edge techniques to develop The Integrated Change System™, earning him the description "the guy that will blow your mind and radically change your life."

Christopher is passionate about pulling people out of their negative patterns of behaviour and showing them how to be free of the emotions that trap them like mental quicksand. His high-energy, fast-paced coaching approach strikes a delicate balance between laser-focused, unconventional, and light-hearted to create change swiftly at an incredibly deep level, ridding his clients of phobias, fears, and anxiety at lightning speed.

When he's not fixing clients, Christopher and his family can be found living their vision of freedom in London and exploring the surrounding countryside with their equally inspired dog Lexi.

READER RESOURCES

Register Your Copy of This Book

To help you implement the strategies in this book, I've shared a range of tools, diagnostics, and checklists that you can download as a reader.

Visit www.FaceYourFearOfFlying.com and register this book to download the toolkit.

Printed in Great Britain
by Amazon